Bridge Without Error

The play of many bridge hands resembles a comedy of errors. A mistake by the declarer is counterbalanced by a defensive slip and the par result is achieved in spite of the worst efforts of all concerned. Mistakes that escape punishment normally go unnoticed and tend to be repeated over and over again. It is only by learning to recognise one's mistakes that a player can hope to improve. The recognition of mistakes is the theme of this quiz book. Adopting a fresh approach, Ron Klinger invites the reader to spot the mistakes that have been made in the course of the bidding, the play and the defence of each hand. All the errors are listed in the solution overleaf, where the picture of the complete deal may be rather different from that shown on the previous page. Given the chance to learn from his mistakes, the reader can hope to avoid some of them in future, thus drawing a little closer to the impossible dream of 'bridge without error'.

One of the top Australian experts, Ron Klinger is also his country's foremost teacher of the game. Those who have read his three previous books on bridge will know that they can rely on him for entertainment combined with sound instruction.

ALSO BY

RON KLINGER

Playing to Win at Bridge
Basic Bridge: A Guide to Good Acol Bidding and Play
Winning Bridge – Trick by Trick

Bridge Without Error

BY

RON KLINGER

LONDON
VICTOR GOLLANCZ LTD
in association with Peter Crawley
1981

I S B N 0 575 02946 3

To
Liz, George and Dan

Typeset by Willmer Brothers Ltd., Birkenhead, Merseyside
Printed in Great Britain by St. Edmundsbury Press Ltd.,
Bury St. Edmunds, Suffolk

INTRODUCTION

Bridge without error is a goal to which we all aspire. In fact it is a fantasy. Even the very best players can produce a flawless session only rarely. Those who regularly claim perfect sessions either delude themselves or find themselves in uncritical or gullible audiences. However it is true to say that the better the player, the fewer the errors. If only we would cut down the number of needless mistakes we make, we would soon find ourselves in strong company. Where the novice might make between 50 and 100 mistakes a session (not all those mistakes cost, thank heavens), the expert would make less than half a dozen.

The aim of this book is to illustrate the countless mistakes that occur in daily play and to demonstrate how they can be eliminated. Before one's errors can disappear they have to be recognised, no easy task for most players. Many contracts and many defences succeed notwithstanding the mistakes that may have been made. Perhaps the cards lay luckily for your side or perhaps the opposition failed to take advantage of your slips. On rarer occasions the best play may fail while an inferior approach would have succeeded.

The arrangement of this quiz book is different from other books of bridge problems. At the start your hand and dummy's is given, together with the bidding and the early play. You are then requested to plan the rest of the play. So far this is familiar and at this stage you should make an earnest endeavour to solve the problem as you would at the table. In particular you should have a concrete idea of how to continue before moving on to the next section. You may assume the bidding is standard unless otherwise stated and standard card play is used (fourth highest leads, king from ace-king, M.U.D., high-low encouraging and high-low for an even number where count is relevant, and so on).

Here is a sample problem:

Rubber bridge ♠ K Q 4 3
East–West vulnerable ♡ A J 4
Dealer North ◇ K 10 7 6 5
♣ 8

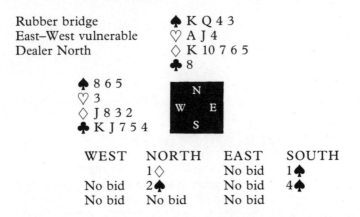

♠ 8 6 5
♡ 3
◇ J 8 3 2
♣ K J 7 5 4

WEST	NORTH	EAST	SOUTH
	1◇	No bid	1♠
No bid	2♠	No bid	4♠
No bid	No bid	No bid	

1. West led the three of hearts: four–**king**–five.
2. East returned the two of hearts: seven–**five of spades**–♡J.

HOW SHOULD WEST CONTINUE?

Note that the card winning the trick appears in **bold** print. Discards appear in *italics*. You might consider the above problem before going on to the next part.

The second and unusual part of each problem is titled HOW THE PLAY WENT. All four hands are shown, followed by a description of how the play proceeded and the outcome. At the end you are asked what errors were committed. Again you should spend some time going over the deal and listing the mistakes you have found before proceeding to the SOLUTION found on the facing page. For the serious player keen to improve, it is a worthwhile exercise to write down the answers to the first two parts of each problem before reading the solution.

Here is Part II of the above problem:

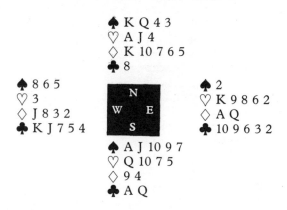

♠ K Q 4 3
♡ A J 4
◇ K 10 7 6 5
♣ 8

♠ 8 6 5
♡ 3
◇ J 8 3 2
♣ K J 7 5 4

♠ 2
♡ K 9 8 6 2
◇ A Q
♣ 10 9 6 3 2

♠ A J 10 9 7
♡ Q 10 7 5
◇ 9 4
♣ A Q

At trick three West led the two of diamonds won by East's ace as dummy played the king. East led a third heart again trumped by West who led another diamond to East's queen and declarer was two down.

WHAT ERRORS, IF ANY, WERE COMMITTED?

You might like to work through Part II before reading on.

The errors may occur in bidding, play or defence, in the early play contained in the first part of the problem or later. You should not assume that because the problem is posed as a defensive problem the errors come in the defence. There may be many errors or there may be none at all, just to keep you on your toes. Do not assume that the model hand under HOW THE PLAY WENT is how the cards actually lay. Finesses that work on the given hand may fail on the actual hand and vice versa; suits that break evenly on the given hand may break badly on the actual hand. Do not assume because a contract succeeds it was played correctly or that because it fails it was defended correctly.

You will come across many bad breaks in the problems as happens in real life. Your plans should always cater for bad breaks as far as possible.

In the SOLUTION you will find comments on the errors made and how they could have been avoided. Usually there will be a slightly different hand diagram, the 'actual hand', showing how the play taken at the table failed to cover some contingency. All the hands occurred at the table, and if you happen to get some wrong you can take comfort from the fact that in practice most of the players faced with the problems also got them wrong.

Here is the solution to the above problem:

Solution:

On the given hand, everyone except dummy fell from grace. On the actual hand declarer in fact succeeded when West returned a diamond at trick three. This was the layout:

7

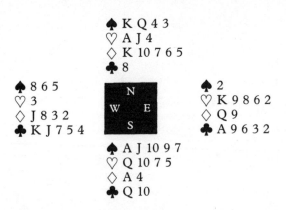

After ♡3 ducked to the king and the ♡2 returned, ruffed, South won the ace of diamonds at trick three, drew the remaining trumps in two rounds, cashed two heart winners to discard a club from dummy and made eleven tricks. The correct defence was for West to switch to a club at trick three to East's ace and a second heart ruff would beat the contract.

On the given hand, East erred by returning the **two** of hearts after winning the ♡K. That play was correct on the above hand where East's entry was clubs but on the earlier hand East should have returned the nine of hearts (high card for the high suit when you know or hope that partner will be ruffing your lead). On the early hand East also erred without cost by not cashing the ◇Q after winning the ◇A (West's ◇2 showed at most four diamonds and it might have been only three – J–x–x – in which case East could have obtained a diamond ruff).

West made a minor mistake ruffing the heart return at trick two with the five of spades. The correct card was the six, intending to high-low in trumps to show an odd number of trumps. The major error was returning a diamond at trick three. East's **two** of hearts asked for a club back.

Declarer also erred. He should not finesse in hearts, but win trick one with the ♡A and draw trumps. He can afford to lose two diamonds and a heart.

Did you find all those mistakes? That was an easy problem and you should not expect to find most of them as straightforward. The problems are not arranged according to theme. They are designed to encourage logical thinking, critical assessment and an appreciation of how the outcome of a hand can be affected by minor differences.

The emphasis throughout is on the practical, day-to-day cares that face us all. I have graded the problems in a rough order of difficulty, the first group being assessed at intermediate level, the middle group at advanced level and the remainder at expert level.

Well, go to it. You are on a search-and-destroy mission. This book is full of mistakes. Your task is to discover and eradicate them. Before you know it they will also be eliminated from your regular game!

INTERMEDIATE LEVEL

DEALS 1 TO 19

1. LET THE PUNISHMENT FIT THE CRIME

♠ K 5   Rubber bridge, both sides vulnerable
♡ 7 2   Dealer North
♢ A Q 4 2
♣ 10 9 8 3 2

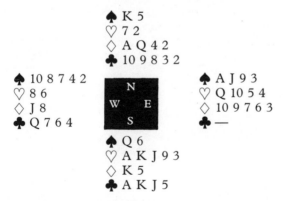

WEST	NORTH	EAST	SOUTH
	No bid	No bid	2NT
No bid	3NT	All pass	

♠ Q 6
♡ A K J 9 3
♢ K 5
♣ A K J 5

No awards for the bidding but the happy-go-lucky approach is typical of the rubber bridge table.
1. West led the four of spades: king–**ace**–six.
2. East returned the jack of spades, won by the **queen** as West followed with the two.
3. South played the **ace of clubs**, *East discarding the* ♠*9*.

HOW SHOULD SOUTH CONTINUE?

HOW THE PLAY WENT:

```
              ♠ K 5
              ♡ 7 2
              ♢ A Q 4 2
              ♣ 10 9 8 3 2
♠ 10 8 7 4 2                  ♠ A J 9 3
♡ 8 6          N             ♡ Q 10 5 4
♢ J 8        W   E           ♢ 10 9 7 6 3
♣ Q 7 6 4       S            ♣ —
              ♠ Q 6
              ♡ A K J 9 3
              ♢ K 5
              ♣ A K J 5
```

After the bad news in the clubs, declarer cashed the king of diamonds and dummy's A–Q of diamonds. The jack of hearts was finessed and declarer made nine tricks via one spade, three hearts, three diamonds and two clubs.

WERE ANY ERRORS COMMITTED?

Solution:
In practice, declarer failed when he took the line stated. This was the actual hand:

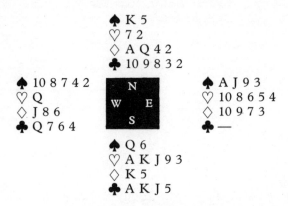

North:
♠ K 5
♡ 7 2
◇ A Q 4 2
♣ 10 9 8 3 2

West:
♠ 10 8 7 4 2
♡ Q
◇ J 8 6
♣ Q 7 6 4

East:
♠ A J 9 3
♡ 10 8 6 5 4
◇ 10 9 7 3
♣ —

South:
♠ Q 6
♡ A K J 9 3
◇ K 5
♣ A K J 5

After winning the second spade, cashing the top club and learning the bad news, declarer should have cashed one top heart before playing off the top three diamonds and taking the heart finesse. (It also would not have hurt to cash the second top club first just in case a careless East discards a diamond from a four-card holding. It is true that few defenders today discard from a suit in which dummy has length when they also hold significant length but if you never set a trap for the opposition, they cannot fall in. It is worth the risk of going down more than one to give yourself a slight extra chance to succeed unless you know the opposition are much too good to let a diamond go from a four-card holding.)

In actual play, declarer neglected to cash one top heart and paid a heavy price later when West won the first heart and cashed his remaining spades. It is true that the chance of a singleton queen is very small but even an extra 2% chance is worth taking since it costs you nothing.

Justice was fully served when East–West made game and rubber on the next hand.

2. WHAT IS THE SET-UP?

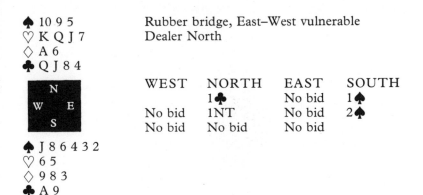

♠ 10 9 5
♡ K Q J 7
◇ A 6
♣ Q J 8 4

Rubber bridge, East–West vulnerable
Dealer North

WEST	NORTH	EAST	SOUTH
	1♣	No bid	1♠
No bid	1NT	No bid	2♠
No bid	No bid	No bid	

♠ J 8 6 4 3 2
♡ 6 5
◇ 9 8 3
♣ A 9

1. West led the three of clubs: **queen**–seven–nine.

HOW SHOULD SOUTH CONTINUE?

HOW THE PLAY WENT:

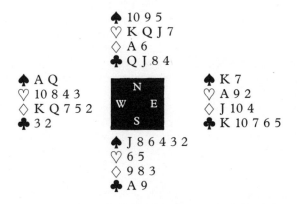

♠ 10 9 5
♡ K Q J 7
◇ A 6
♣ Q J 8 4

♠ A Q
♡ 10 8 4 3
◇ K Q 7 5 2
♣ 3 2

♠ K 7
♡ A 9 2
◇ J 10 4
♣ K 10 7 6 5

♠ J 8 6 4 3 2
♡ 6 5
◇ 9 8 3
♣ A 9

At trick two, a trump was led from dummy, seven, eight, queen. The ♣2 was continued, four, five, ace. A second round of trumps cleared that suit and declarer lost just two spades, a heart and a diamond. Making three.

WERE THERE ANY MISTAKES?

Solution:

South's play was very dangerous at trick two. At trick four, when in with the ace of clubs, declarer again could have recovered but the second round of trumps while successful on the given hand cost the contract on the actual hand which looked like this:

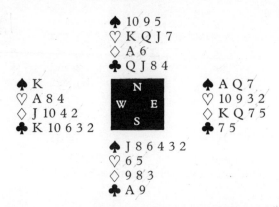

                    ♠ 10 9 5
                    ♡ K Q J 7
                    ◇ A 6
                    ♣ Q J 8 4

♠ K   ♠ A Q 7
♡ A 8 4   N   ♡ 10 9 3 2
◇ J 10 4 2 W   E   ◇ K Q 7 5
♣ K 10 6 3 2   S   ♣ 7 5

                    ♠ J 8 6 4 3 2
                    ♡ 6 5
                    ◇ 9 8 3
                    ♣ A 9

West might have led a diamond initially but in fact chose the club. With dummy's ♣Q winning, declarer led a spade to West's king. Back came a club won by South and again a trump was led, East winning and cashing the third round of trumps. Then came the diamond switch and declarer could no longer avoid losing three spades, a heart and two diamonds.

South could have saved the position at trick four by leading a heart. If West took the ace, declarer would in fact have two discards on the hearts. If West ducked, best, dummy would win and should continue with another top heart, thus establishing a heart winner for a diamond discard and securing the contract.

In fact, declarer should have led a heart from dummy at trick two. While this does not guarantee the contract, it is easily the best line. It is important to set up an extra winner in hearts while the ace of diamonds is still there as an entry. It is not as good to lead a low diamond from dummy at trick two, planning to take a diamond ruff. It may be possible for an opponent to win the diamond, play A–K–Q of spades and then knock out the ◇A before the ♡A has been knocked out.

On the actual hand above, after winning the ♠K, West can defeat the contract with a diamond lead. East can obtain the lead in diamonds, draw dummy's trumps and continue the diamonds.

3. TAKE YOUR ORDER, SIR

♠ A K 6 5
♡ 10 4 3
◇ A Q J 7 2
♣ 6

Rubber bridge, North–South vulnerable
Dealer South

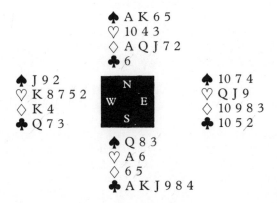

SOUTH	WEST	NORTH	EAST
1♣	No bid	1◇	No bid
3♣	No bid	3♠	No bid
3NT	No bid	No bid	No bid

♠ Q 8 3
♡ A 6
◇ 6 5
♣ A K J 9 8 4

1. West led the five of hearts: three–**nine**–six.
2. East continued with the ♡Q: **ace**–two–four.

HOW SHOULD SOUTH PLAN THE PLAY?

HOW THE PLAY WENT:

```
                 ♠ A K 6 5
                 ♡ 10 4 3
                 ◇ A Q J 7 2
                 ♣ 6
   ♠ J 9 2              N           ♠ 10 7 4
   ♡ K 8 7 5 2       W     E        ♡ Q J 9
   ◇ K 4                            ◇ 10 9 8 3
   ♣ Q 7 3              S           ♣ 10 5 2
                 ♠ Q 8 3
                 ♡ A 6
                 ◇ 6 5
                 ♣ A K J 9 8 4
```

After winning the ace of hearts, South took the diamond finesse successfully. He returned to the queen of spades and led another diamond, capturing West's king with the ace. When the jack of diamonds failed to draw the remaining diamonds declarer finessed the jack of clubs. West took the queen of clubs and cashed three more hearts, defeating 3NT by one trick.

WHAT ERRORS WERE COMMITTED?

Solution:

South's error in finessing the jack of clubs was, of course, puerile. After three diamond tricks were in the bag, declarer had nine top tricks and when the spades were 3–3, declarer could have made an overtrick without risk. No competent player would go down once there were nine tricks for the taking.

However, a number of players would make the error of technique committed by South earlier in the hand. If your answer referred only to the club finesse error, check again before consulting the solution below.

Declarer did indeed go one down on the hand but a lot sooner for the actual hand looked like this:

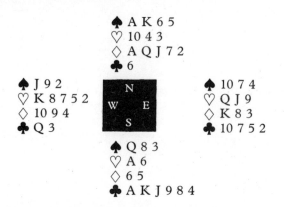

♠ A K 6 5
♡ 10 4 3
◇ A Q J 7 2
♣ 6

♠ J 9 2
♡ K 8 7 5 2
◇ 10 9 4
♣ Q 3

♠ 10 7 4
♡ Q J 9
◇ K 8 3
♣ 10 7 5 2

♠ Q 8 3
♡ A 6
◇ 6 5
♣ A K J 9 8 4

After declarer won the ace of hearts at trick two, he did take the diamond finesse which was unsuccessful. East won the king and returned the jack of hearts, West naturally overtaking with the king to cash his remaining hearts for one down.

Taking the diamond finesse early was an error in timing. If the diamond finesse is working, one can still take it later and declarer can increase his chance of success by trying first a line which will not lose the lead if unsuccessful. With seven top tricks, declarer cannot succeed merely by producing another spade trick but he can eliminate the need for the diamond finesse if he can produce two extra black winners.

The best line after winning the ♡A is to cash the ace and king of clubs. Then, if the ♣Q has dropped, cash the jack of clubs and the ace, king and queen of spades in that order. If the spades turn out to be 3–3, cross to the ◇A to cash the good spade while if spades do not break, you are in hand with the ♠Q to take the diamond finesse.

If the ♣Q does not drop in two rounds, revert to taking the diamond finesse at once, using the ♠Q as the next entry to repeat the diamond finesse.

4. ONE-WAY STREET

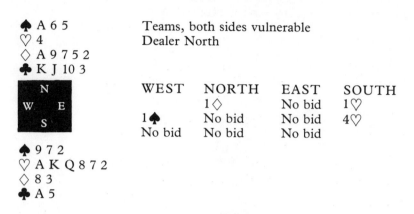

♠ A 6 5
♡ 4
◇ A 9 7 5 2
♣ K J 10 3

Teams, both sides vulnerable
Dealer North

WEST	NORTH	EAST	SOUTH
	1◇	No bid	1♡
1♠	No bid	No bid	4♡
No bid	No bid	No bid	

♠ 9 7 2
♡ A K Q 8 7 2
◇ 8 3
♣ A 5

1. West led the king of spades: **ace**–four–two.
2. Four of hearts from dummy: three–**ace**–six.
3. **King** of hearts led: nine–◇2–five of hearts.
4. **Queen** of hearts led: *West discards* ♠8– ◇5 from dummy–♡10.

HOW SHOULD SOUTH CONTINUE?

HOW THE PLAY WENT:

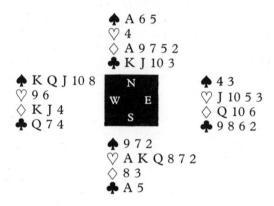

♠ A 6 5
♡ 4
◇ A 9 7 5 2
♣ K J 10 3

♠ K Q J 10 8
♡ 9 6
◇ K J 4
♣ Q 7 4

♠ 4 3
♡ J 10 5 3
◇ Q 10 6
♣ 9 8 6 2

♠ 9 7 2
♡ A K Q 8 7 2
◇ 8 3
♣ A 5

At trick five, South played the ace of clubs and followed with a club to the jack which held. The king of clubs allowed one spade discard and as the queen luckily fell, declarer was able to discard the other spade loser on the ten of clubs. He conceded a heart and a diamond, making five.

WERE THERE ANY ERRORS?

Solution:

Declarer committed a serious error which cost the contract on the actual hand, whereas the contract was unbeatable unless East happened to be extremely short in the minors. This was the layout:

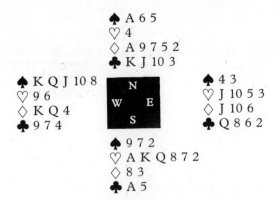

```
                    ♠ A 6 5
                    ♡ 4
                    ◇ A 9 7 5 2
                    ♣ K J 10 3
♠ K Q J 10 8                         ♠ 4 3
♡ 9 6             N                  ♡ J 10 5 3
◇ K Q 4       W        E             ◇ J 10 6
♣ 9 7 4           S                  ♣ Q 8 6 2
                    ♠ 9 7 2
                    ♡ A K Q 8 7 2
                    ◇ 8 3
                    ♣ A 5
```

South correctly won the first spade. It would have been foolish to duck the first spade and find the ace of spades is ruffed at trick two when West started with six spades. After the three top hearts, declarer erred by taking the direct club finesse. East won the queen and returned a spade, declarer thus losing four tricks.

This was more than merely bad luck that the ♣Q was with East rather than West. Declarer can almost guarantee the contract by playing ace of clubs, a club to the king and then leading the jack of clubs for a ruffing finesse.

If on the above hand, East covers with the queen of clubs, declarer ruffs and later discards a loser on the ten of clubs. If East ducks the jack, declarer discards a spade as the jack takes the trick. If on the other hand (the one on the previous page) the queen of clubs is with West, South still discards a spade on the ♣J. West can win the queen of clubs and cash a spade but declarer loses just the jack of hearts extra, as the losing diamond goes away on the now established ten of clubs.

5. ALL RISKS POLICY

Teams both sides vulnerable
Dealer North

	♠ 9 7 5 2
	♡ J 3
	◇ Q J 9
	♣ A J 10 4

WEST	NORTH	EAST	SOUTH
	Pass	1♡	2♠(1)
Pass	4♠	All pass	

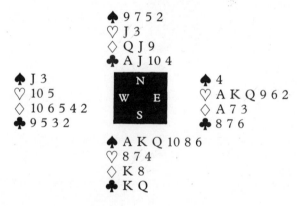

♠ 4
♡ A K Q 9 6 2
◇ A 7 3
♣ 8 7 6

(1) Strong, 15+ points, 5+ suit.

1. West led the ten of hearts: three . . .

HOW SHOULD EAST PLAN THE DEFENCE?

HOW THE PLAY WENT:

```
                 ♠ 9 7 5 2
                 ♡ J 3
                 ◇ Q J 9
                 ♣ A J 10 4
   ♠ J 3              N          ♠ 4
   ♡ 10 5        W        E      ♡ A K Q 9 6 2
   ◇ 10 6 5 4 2      S          ◇ A 7 3
   ♣ 9 5 3 2                     ♣ 8 7 6
                 ♠ A K Q 10 8 6
                 ♡ 8 7 4
                 ◇ K 8
                 ♣ K Q
```

1. East encouraged the hearts with the ♡9.
2. West led a second heart won by East's queen.
3. East led the ace of hearts, West trumping with the jack and the ♣4 being discarded from dummy.
4. West returned a diamond to East's ace.

ONE DOWN –

WHAT ERRORS WERE COMMITTED?

Solution:
On the given hand there were two minor errors:
(1) East should have overtaken the ♡10 with the queen at trick one. West's ♡10 was obviously a singleton or a doubleton (East's ♡9 precluded a sequence lead) and if it were a singleton it may not have been obvious to West to switch to a diamond rather than a club.
(2) Declarer should have discarded a diamond from dummy, not the ♣4. While West ought to find the diamond return at trick four, declarer needs to keep four clubs in dummy to have any chance of making the contract. If West errs and brings back a black card, South wins, draws trumps and overtakes the second club in dummy, using dummy's *two extra* clubs to discard two diamonds. If one of dummy's clubs is discarded, declarer has no chance.

On the actual layout however, East's defence allowed declarer to make with an overtrick? This was the hand:

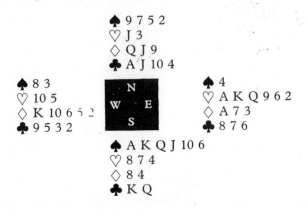

♠ 9 7 5 2
♡ J 3
◇ Q J 9
♣ A J 10 4

♠ 8 3
♡ 10 5
◇ K 10 6 5 2
♣ 9 5 3 2

♠ 4
♡ A K Q 9 6 2
◇ A 7 3
♣ 8 7 6

♠ A K Q J 10 6
♡ 8 7 4
◇ 8 4
♣ K Q

East won the second heart but West could not overruff dummy on the third heart. Dummy ruffed, declarer drew trumps and the two diamond losers disappeared on the clubs. Making five.

The correct defence is for East to win the first heart, cash a second top heart and then cash the ace of diamonds. If West encourages diamonds, East can play a second diamond, as on the hand above. Where West has a trump higher than dummy's, West will discourage diamonds and East can then revert to hearts. Cashing the diamond ace first followed by the heart ruff also eliminates any risk of West failing to guess the diamond return after the heart ruff.

6. ENTER AT YOUR OWN RISK

♠ Q 9 5　　　　　Rubber bridge, neither side vulnerable
♡ J 7 4 3 2　　　Dealer South
◇ A Q 3
♣ 6 5

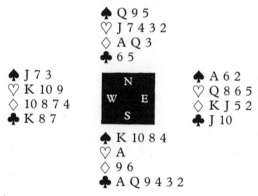

SOUTH	WEST	NORTH	EAST
1♣	No bid	1♡	No bid
1♠	No bid	1NT	No bid
2♣	No bid	No bid	No bid

♠ K 10 8 4
♡ A
◇ 9 6
♣ A Q 9 4 3 2

1. West led the four of diamonds: queen–**king**–six.
2. East switched to the five of hearts: **ace**–ten–two.
3. South cashed the **ace** of clubs: seven–five–ten.

DO YOU AGREE WITH THE PLAY SO FAR?

HOW SHOULD SOUTH CONTINUE?

HOW THE PLAY WENT:

　　　　　　　♠ Q 9 5
　　　　　　　♡ J 7 4 3 2
　　　　　　　◇ A Q 3
　　　　　　　♣ 6 5

♠ J 7 3　　　　　　　　　　　♠ A 6 2
♡ K 10 9　　　　　　　　　　♡ Q 8 6 5
◇ 10 8 7 4　　　　　　　　　◇ K J 5 2
♣ K 8 7　　　　　　　　　　 ♣ J 10

　　　　　　　♠ K 10 8 4
　　　　　　　♡ A
　　　　　　　◇ 9 6
　　　　　　　♣ A Q 9 4 3 2

After the ten of clubs dropped at trick three, declarer decided to avoid a guess and crossed to dummy's ace of diamonds to lead the second club. When East produced the jack, South covered with the queen and West won the king. West led a third round of diamonds, but South ruffed, drew the last trump and led a spade to the nine. When this forced the ace, South had made two overtricks.

WHAT MISTAKES, IF ANY, WERE MADE?

Solution:

Declarer in fact failed in two clubs for the complete hand was as follows:

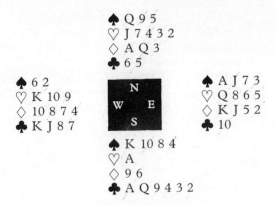

♠ Q 9 5
♡ J 7 4 3 2
◇ A Q 3
♣ 6 5

♠ 6 2
♡ K 10 9
◇ 10 8 7 4
♣ K J 8 7

♠ A J 7 3
♡ Q 8 6 5
◇ K J 5 2
♣ 10

♠ K 10 8 4
♡ A
◇ 9 6
♣ A Q 9 4 3 2

After the ◇4 lead, queen, king, East returned a heart to South's ace. The ♣A dropped East's ten and when declarer crossed to the ◇A to lead the second club, he discovered he had three club losers. Furthermore, he was unable to return to dummy and could not play the spades without losing two tricks.

After the ♣A, declarer should have continued with a low club from hand. The contract is always safe on a 3–2 club break; at worst declarer can lose two clubs, two spades and a diamond. When West's club holding reveals three trump losers, declarer has not wasted his ◇A entry and he can use that later to play the spades. As East has shown up with short clubs, it is logical to play him for length in spades and hence the jack of spades. As it happens, the percentage play in spades works.

As for the early play, it was reasonable for South to try the diamond finesse at trick one. To refuse the finesse incurs a risk of creating a certain diamond loser as well as five possible black losers. East, however, after winning the king of diamonds should have returned a diamond. West's lead of the four, his lowest, showed an honour card under normal methods and thus it was safe for East to return a diamond as the ten had to be with West. Upon winning the ace of diamonds, declarer would have had no grounds to lead a spade to his ten there and then and if he failed to do that, he would also fail in his contract.

7. HEAR A PIN DROP

♠ A Q 8 7 4　　　Rubber bridge, East–West +60,
♡ J 10 2　　　　neither side vulnerable
◇ A　　　　　　Dealer North
♣ J 10 3 2

WEST	NORTH	EAST	SOUTH
	1♠	No bid	2◇
No bid	2♠	No bid	5◇
No bid	No bid	No bid	

♠ 5
♡ A
◇ Q 10 9 8 6 5 3
♣ K Q 6 4

1. West led the **ace** of clubs: two–seven–four.
2. West led the five of clubs: three–eight–**king**.
3. South led the three of diamonds: four–**ace**–seven.
4. The two of hearts from dummy: four–**ace**–five.

HOW SHOULD SOUTH CONTINUE?

HOW THE PLAY WENT:

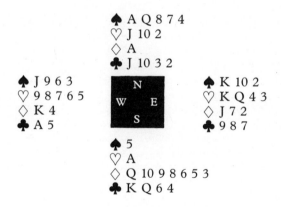

At trick five South led the ◇8, West winning with the king.

West switched to the three of spades, taken by the ace. A second spade was ruffed with the ten of diamonds followed by the queen of diamonds, drawing the jack. Making five diamonds.

WHAT ERRORS WERE COMMITTED?

Solution:
Five clubs although no certainty, is a better spot than five diamonds and South might have shown his clubs rather than leap to the diamond game. In five diamonds, declarer in fact failed on his line when the layout looked like this:

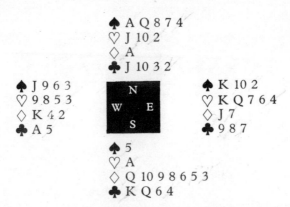

After West led ace and another club and South cashed the ◇A and crossed to the ♡A, declarer's ten of diamonds was ducked to the jack and declarer conceded one down. Superficially, it may look as though it is a straight guess whether to play for a doubleton king (lead low diamond) or a doubleton jack (lead the queen to pin the jack, the winning play on the actual hand). However there are a number of reasons why the queen play, though not assured of success, is the better chance.

Firstly, West's lead of ace and another club, looking for a ruff, is more likely to include a trump holding of K–x–x rather than K–x. The best singleton or doubleton leads are when a defender has control in trumps (ace or king) and *a spare trump* for ruffing.

Secondly, as the king-doubleton or jack-doubleton holding in diamonds is equally likely mathematically, you should play for the situation which guarantees success if it works. Thus if you lead the queen and this does pin the jack the hand is over. If however, you lead low and find that you do drop the king doubleton you may still fail because of the possibility of a club ruff. Suppose in the above hand the king and jack of diamonds are interchanged. Now you cannot succeed by dropping the doubleton king as West still obtains the club ruff. Why play for a situation which can rarely gain?

8. HEARTBREAKING EXPERIENCE

♠ 8 7 6
♡ 5 4 3
◇ K 7 6 5
♣ K 5 4

Rubber bridge, neither side vulnerable
Dealer North

WEST	NORTH	EAST	SOUTH
	No bid	No bid	1♣
No bid	1◇	1♠	2♡
No bid	3♣	All pass	

♠ J 2
♡ A K 7 2
◇ A 4
♣ A 8 7 6 2

1. West led the three of clubs . . .

HOW SHOULD SOUTH PLAN THE PLAY?

HOW THE PLAY WENT:

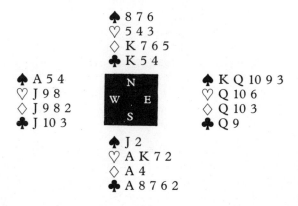

```
                ♠ 8 7 6
                ♡ 5 4 3
                ◇ K 7 6 5
                ♣ K 5 4
♠ A 5 4                        ♠ K Q 10 9 3
♡ J 9 8          N             ♡ Q 10 6
◇ J 9 8 2     W     E          ◇ Q 10 3
♣ J 10 3         S             ♣ Q 9
                ♠ J 2
                ♡ A K 7 2
                ◇ A 4
                ♣ A 8 7 6 2
```

Declarer won the ace and king of clubs and then played ace, king and another heart. East won the heart but declarer was home, conceding just two spades, a heart and a club.

WERE THERE ANY MISTAKES?

Solution:
Three clubs is a very delicate contract which cannot stand any violently nasty breaks, as declarer has inevitably two spades, one heart and one club to lose. If clubs are 3–2 and hearts 3–3, declarer never has any problems. However, declarer should try to cope with a 4–2 break in hearts, the most common division when six cards are missing in the suit.

The fact that a club was led indicates that clubs probably are breaking (there is nothing declarer can do if they do not break) and also suggests that hearts probably are not 3–3. The likelihood is that West has a strongish holding in hearts which has made him prefer the trump lead to leading his partner's suit. That was the case on the actual hand when declarer failed by taking the given line:

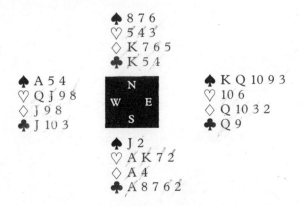

West led the three of clubs, (the standard lead from J–10–x is the low card) and South won the ace and king of clubs. However, after ace, king and another heart, West won the jack of hearts, cashed the jack of clubs, drawing dummy's trump, and followed with the queen of hearts. As East had signalled for spades, West then led the ace of spades and a second spade defeated the contract.

Note that it would not have helped declarer to win the first club with the ace (or king) and play ace, king and a third heart before drawing the second round of trumps. West would win the third heart and play the fourth heart: then if declarer trumped low, East would overtrump while if declarer trumped with the king of clubs, that would set up two trump winners for the defence.

The winning play, easy enough to overlook, which caters for hearts 3–3 or 4–2 and clubs 3–2, is to win the king of clubs and duck a heart. When South regains the lead, the ♣A is taken followed by ace, king and the last heart, trumping it in dummy if necessary. If clubs are 3–2, the opponents can trump in on hearts only with their master trump.

9. PRIMARY INDUSTRY

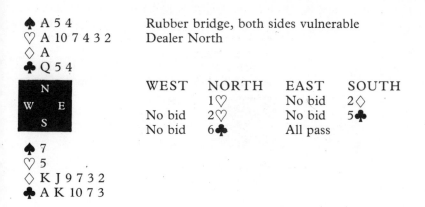

♠ A 5 4
♡ A 10 7 4 3 2
◇ A
♣ Q 5 4

Rubber bridge, both sides vulnerable
Dealer North

WEST	NORTH	EAST	SOUTH
	1♡	No bid	2◇
No bid	2♡	No bid	5♣
No bid	6♣	All pass	

♠ 7
♡ 5
◇ K J 9 7 3 2
♣ A K 10 7 3

1. West led the queen of spades . . .

HOW SHOULD SOUTH PLAN THE PLAY?

HOW THE PLAY WENT:

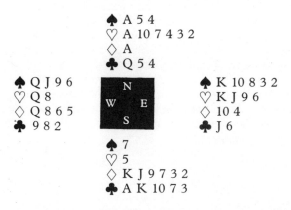

♠ A 5 4
♡ A 10 7 4 3 2
◇ A
♣ Q 5 4

♠ Q J 9 6
♡ Q 8
◇ Q 8 6 5
♣ 9 8 2

♠ K 10 8 3 2
♡ K J 9 6
◇ 10 4
♣ J 6

♠ 7
♡ 5
◇ K J 9 7 3 2
♣ A K 10 7 3

Declarer won the ace of spades and cashed the ace of diamonds. He then ruffed a spade and ruffed a low diamond in dummy. Trumps were drawn and when the queen of diamonds did not drop under the king, declarer conceded a diamond and made twelve tricks.

WHAT ERRORS WERE COMMITTED?

Solution:
Declarer went one off in his slam when he played the hand as stated. The actual hand looked like this:

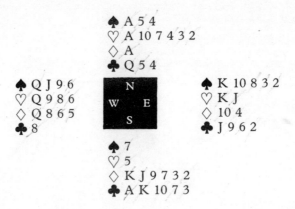

```
                    ♠ A 5 4
                    ♡ A 10 7 4 3 2
                    ◇ A
                    ♣ Q 5 4
  ♠ Q J 9 6                          ♠ K 10 8 3 2
  ♡ Q 9 8 6         N                ♡ K J
  ◇ Q 8 6 5      W     E             ◇ 10 4
  ♣ 8               S                ♣ J 9 6 2
                    ♠ 7
                    ♡ 5
                    ◇ K J 9 7 3 2
                    ♣ A K 10 7 3
```

After winning ♠A and ◇A, ruffing a spade and ruffing a diamond in dummy, declarer played the queen of clubs and a club to his ace. When the bad club break appeared, declarer could not avoid losing a club trick and when the diamonds were not 3–3, declarer also had to lose a trick to the queen of diamonds for one down.

Declarer can cope with these bad breaks by means of a simple precaution. Instead of using a spade ruff to reach hand at trick three he should use a trump entry. The play would go: ♠A, ◇A, ♣Q, club to the ace . . . Now if clubs are 3–2, declarer can ruff a low diamond, ruff a spade back to hand, draw the remaining trump and, if necessary, concede a diamond. When the bad club break appears, declarer is able to cope with J–x–x–x with East by crossing to the ace of hearts and finessing the ten of clubs. The last trump is drawn and declarer continues with king and another diamond, succeeding if diamonds are 3–3 or if there is a doubleton ten or doubleton queen.

10. A LEADING QUESTION

Rubber bridge, North–South vulnerable and +40: East–West +90; Dealer South

SOUTH	WEST	NORTH	EAST
1NT	2♠	Double	3♣
3◇	No bid	No bid	No bid

What should West lead from:

♠ Q 10 9 7 6 5 2
♡ 9 8 3
◇ A 10
♣ 8

HOW THE PLAY WENT:

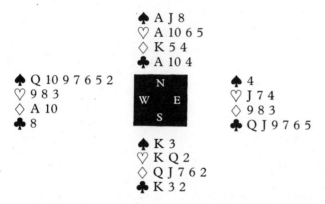

♠ A J 8
♡ A 10 6 5
◇ K 5 4
♣ A 10 4

♠ Q 10 9 7 6 5 2   ♠ 4
♡ 9 8 3   ♡ J 7 4
◇ A 10   ◇ 9 8 3
♣ 8   ♣ Q J 9 7 6 5

♠ K 3
♡ K Q 2
◇ Q J 7 6 2
♣ K 3 2

West led the eight of clubs won by South's king. South led a trump and West rose with the ace to lead a spade. The jack of spades held the trick, trumps were drawn and declarer made twelve tricks for game and rubber.

WHAT ERRORS, IF ANY, WERE COMMITTED?

Solution:
In the bidding South should have left 3♣ to partner. If partner could make a penalty double, South would be pleased indeed. On the actual hand 3◇ could have been a very expensive decision if West had found the best defence. This was the hand:

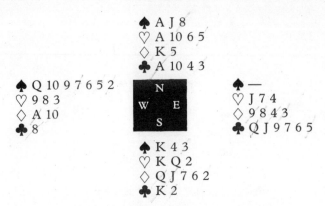

The killing defence: West leads the *two* of spades, ruffed by East. Reading the suit-preference implications of the lead, East would return a club. South would win and lead a trump but West would rise with the ace, give East another spade ruff, receive a club ruff, and a third spade ruff would spell one down.

That lead is not too hard to find since East would be odds on to have a spade void (North's penalty double would often be based on four spades and East's run to 3♣ also suggests a void in spades).

Had that defence been found, North–South might have pursued a discussion whereby South would have conceded that it would have been better to allow North to double 3♣ (the carnage would have been bloody) and North would have admitted that with such a hefty point count 3NT would have been safer than to leave 3◇ in with no fit and wild hands about from the East–West bidding.

11. SPEED KILLS

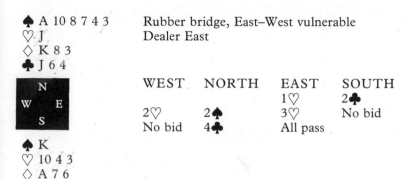

♠ A 10 8 7 4 3
♡ J
◇ K 8 3
♣ J 6 4

Rubber bridge, East–West vulnerable
Dealer East

WEST	NORTH	EAST	SOUTH
		1♡	2♣
2♡	2♠	3♡	No bid
No bid	4♣	All pass	

♠ K
♡ 10 4 3
◇ A 7 6
♣ K 9 8 7 5 3

1. West led the five of hearts: jack–**ace**–three.
2. East returned the four of diamonds . . .

HOW SHOULD SOUTH PLAN THE PLAY?

HOW THE PLAY WENT:

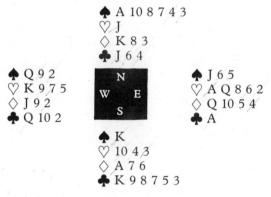

♠ A 10 8 7 4 3
♡ J
◇ K 8 3
♣ J 6 4

♠ Q 9 2
♡ K 9 7 5
◇ J 9 2
♣ Q 10 2

♠ J 6 5
♡ A Q 8 6 2
◇ Q 10 5 4
♣ A

♠ K
♡ 10 4 3
◇ A 7 6
♣ K 9 8 7 5 3

2. . . . South won the ace of diamonds.
3. The ♠K was cashed.
4. A heart was ruffed in dummy.
5. The ♠A allowed a diamond discard.
6. The ◇K was cashed.
7. A diamond was ruffed by declarer.
8. The last heart was ruffed in dummy.
9. The ♣J was led, taken by the ace.
   The defence took one more club trick but declarer made 4♣.

WHAT ERRORS WERE COMMITTED?

Solution:
Declarer failed on the given line when a bad break allowed the defence to make three trump tricks on this layout:

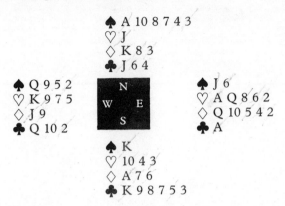

♠ A 10 8 7 4 3
♡ J
◇ K 8 3
♣ J 6 4

♠ Q 9 5 2
♡ K 9 7 5
◇ J 9
♣ Q 10 2

♠ J 6
♡ A Q 8 6 2
◇ Q 10 5 4 2
♣ A

♠ K
♡ 10 4 3
◇ A 7 6
♣ K 9 8 7 5 3

After the ♡A, East's diamond switch was won by the ace. The ♠K was followed by a heart ruff and a diamond was discarded on the ♠A. Then came the king of diamonds and a third diamond ruffed by South. However, West overruffed and when East came in with the ♣A, another diamond promoted West's ♣Q.

There was no need for South to cash the ♠K early or to take the diamond discard early. After winning the ◇A, South should ruff a heart at once, cross back to the ♠K and ruff the third heart. Then the ♣J from dummy allows declarer to succeed on the given layout and whenever he reasonably can.

If East were to follow with the ♣2 on the jack, declarer may have to guess the club position, the odds favouring rising with the ♣K in view of East's opening and the ♡K apparently being with West. To duck the ♣J to West's queen could be expensive if West held Q–10 and East the A–2. West would win and lead a second diamond. If the ◇K is followed by the ♠A for a diamond pitch and a third spade, East could ruff the spade with ♣A and lead another diamond to promote West's queen.

12. SECOND STRING

♠ K
♡ K 8 3 2
◇ K 10 7 5 4
♣ 8 4 3

Match points, neither side vulnerable
Dealer South

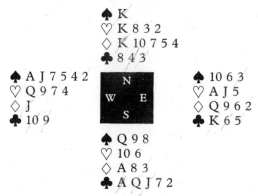

SOUTH	WEST	NORTH	EAST
1♣	1♠	Double(1)	No bid
1NT	No bid	No bid	No bid

♠ Q 9 8
♡ 10 6
◇ A 8 3
♣ A Q J 7 2

(1) Negative Double.
1. West led ♠5: **king**–three–eight.

HOW SHOULD SOUTH PLAN THE PLAY
Suppose the play went:
2. Three of clubs from dummy: five–**queen**–nine.

HOW SHOULD DECLARER NOW PROCEED?

HOW THE PLAY WENT:

```
              ♠ K
              ♡ K 8 3 2
              ◇ K 10 7 5 4
              ♣ 8 4 3
♠ A J 7 5 4 2         ♠ 10 6 3
♡ Q 9 7 4             ♡ A J 5
◇ J                   ◇ Q 9 6 2
♣ 10 9               ♣ K 6 5
              ♠ Q 9 8
              ♡ 10 6
              ◇ A 8 3
              ♣ A Q J 7 2
```

The king of spades won the first trick and a low club went to South's queen. A low diamond to dummy's king and another club finesse brought declarer up to eight tricks but that was all. East later gained the lead to put a spade through South.

WHAT MISTAKES, IF ANY, WERE MADE?

Solution:
By missing a slight improvement declarer in fact failed when the layout was like this:

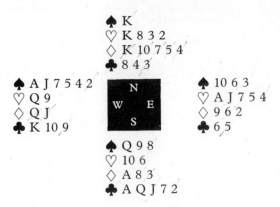

♠ K
♥ K 8 3 2
♦ K 10 7 5 4
♣ 8 4 3

♠ A J 7 5 4 2
♥ Q 9
♦ Q J
♣ K 10 9

♠ 10 6 3
♥ A J 7 5 4
♦ 9 6 2
♣ 6 5

♠ Q 9 8
♥ 10 6
♦ A 8 3
♣ A Q J 7 2

The ♠K won and declarer successfully finessed the queen of clubs. A low diamond to dummy's king and a second club finesse spelt doom for South. West took the king of clubs and switched to the queen of hearts, king, ace. The jack of hearts was cashed and then a spade gave the defence another five tricks for down two.

Although repeating the club finesse looks normal, declarer could have given himself a slight extra chance. At trick three, instead of a low diamond to the king, he could play ace and another diamond to dummy. On the above layout he would then have five diamond tricks and he could take the club finesse later if it appeared warranted.

West could have taken the first club and switched to hearts to defeat the contract but West was not sure which red suit to test. Hence he decided to let the first club win, confident that South would return to dummy for another club finesse. Once West saw which suit provided declarer's entry to dummy, he would know to switch to the other suit to find East's entry.

♠ A 10 8 7 6
♡ K 5
◇ 10 8 6
♣ 8 6 3

Rubber bridge, neither side vulnerable
Dealer South

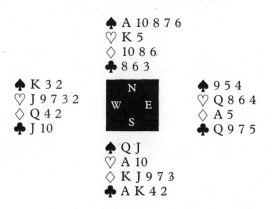

SOUTH	WEST	NORTH	EAST
1◇	No bid	1♠	No bid
2NT	No bid	3NT	All pass

♠ Q J
♡ A 10
◇ K J 9 7 3
♣ A K 4 2

1. West led the three of hearts . . .

HOW SHOULD SOUTH PLAN THE PLAY?

HOW THE PLAY WENT:

```
              ♠ A 10 8 7 6
              ♡ K 5
              ◇ 10 8 6
              ♣ 8 6 3
♠ K 3 2                      ♠ 9 5 4
♡ J 9 7 3 2    N             ♡ Q 8 6 4
◇ Q 4 2     W     E          ◇ A 5
♣ J 10         S             ♣ Q 9 7 5
              ♠ Q J
              ♡ A 10
              ◇ K J 9 7 3
              ♣ A K 4 2
```

South let the heart lead run to his ace, East playing the queen. The queen of spades was led, West ducked and the queen won the trick. The jack of spades won the next trick, West ducking again. Declarer crossed to dummy with the king of hearts and cashed the spade tricks. Making 3NT with five spades, two hearts and two clubs.

WERE THERE ANY ERRORS?

Solution:
Declarer failed when he took the stated line, even though the spade finesse worked. This was the complete hand:

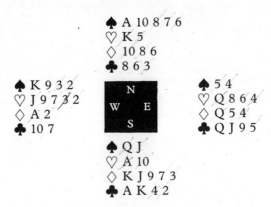

♠ A 10 8 7 6
♥ K 5
♦ 10 8 6
♣ 8 6 3

♠ K 9 3 2
♥ J 9 7 3 2
♦ A 2
♣ 10 7

♠ 5 4
♥ Q 8 6 4
♦ Q 5 4
♣ Q J 9 5

♠ Q J
♥ A 10
♦ K J 9 7 3
♣ A K 4 2

Declarer won the first heart with the ace and ran the queen of spades. The jack of spades followed, West again playing low and the jack winning. Declarer crossed to the king of hearts and played the ace of spades but when the king of spades did not fall, declarer had to lose a spade, a diamond and three hearts.

The correct line of play is to win the first heart in dummy and take the diamond finesse, leading any diamond from dummy and letting it run if East plays low. West wins the ♦A and plays a second heart won by South who now leads the queen of spades to dummy's ace (whether or not the king is played) to repeat the diamond finesse as often as necessary, leading dummy's diamond pip and playing low from hand unless the queen appears from East.

The spade play and the diamond play both fail if the key card is wrong, but the spade play will also fail when the key card is right, unless West holds precisely K–x–x or K–9 doubleton. If West holds K–x–x–x or K–x–x–x–x or K–singleton or K–x and covers the first spade, South cannot come home via the spade suit. (If West has K–x and covers the second spade, declarer can test the ten of spades and revert to diamonds if spades do not behave.)

By contrast, the diamond play will work whether East has Q bare, Q-doubleton, Q–x–x or Q–x–x–x (even A–Q–x–x–x if the spade finesse is on). You may not win on every hand but in the long run following the line with the best chance will put you in front.

14. SWITCH OFF

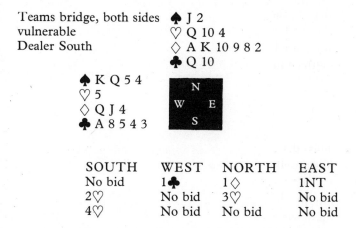

Teams bridge, both sides vulnerable
Dealer South

♠ J 2
♡ Q 10 4
◇ A K 10 9 8 2
♣ Q 10

♠ K Q 5 4
♡ 5
◇ Q J 4
♣ A 8 5 4 3

SOUTH	WEST	NORTH	EAST
No bid	1♣	1◇	1NT
2♡	No bid	3♡	No bid
4♡	No bid	No bid	No bid

1. West led the **ace** of clubs: ten–six–nine.

HOW SHOULD WEST CONTINUE?

HOW THE PLAY WENT:

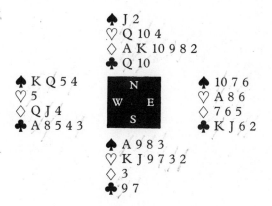

♠ J 2
♡ Q 10 4
◇ A K 10 9 8 2
♣ Q 10

♠ K Q 5 4
♡ 5
◇ Q J 4
♣ A 8 5 4 3

♠ 10 7 6
♡ A 8 6
◇ 7 6 5
♣ K J 6 2

♠ A 9 8 3
♡ K J 9 7 3 2
◇ 3
♣ 9 7

At trick two, West switched to the king of spades, won by the ace. Declarer crossed to the ◇A and pitched his club loser on the ◇K. He then conceded the ♠J to West. West led a club but South ruffed, ruffed a spade, ruffed a diamond high and ruffed his last spade. The ♡A was lost but declarer had ten tricks.

WHAT ERRORS WERE COMMITTED?

Solution:

After the hand was over, West apologised:

"Sorry, partner. I could not read the *six* of clubs. I was afraid that South might have J–9–7 and you the K–6–2 and that if I continued clubs the jack with South would set up and allow a spade discard from dummy. For instance, if South held ♠ A x x ♡ K J x x x x ◇ x ♣ J x x, it would be fatal to play a second club. Another problem was that your six might have been from J–7–6 and that we could cash two spades only if we did it right away."

East replied in similar vein:

"Sorry, partner. I wanted to encourage the club continuation by playing the jack but I felt that could be too expensive. For instance, if you held A–x–x–x and South held 9–x–x, by signalling with the jack, I would be setting up South's nine as a winner if clubs were continued."

IS THERE A WAY THAT EAST–WEST MIGHT HAVE RESOLVED THIS PROBLEM?

Had West known that East held four clubs West would have had no problem in finding the club continuation. The problem arose from East's eccentric choice of 1NT over 1◇. Had East made a normal raise of 2♣ promising length in clubs (it is dangerous to raise *clubs* on three card support), the defence would have had no problem in finding ♣A and a second club, followed by the spade switch to ensure one down.

West made another error later in the play. After winning the ♠Q at trick five, it was futile to play a club. It should have been obvious that South was out of clubs. Had West switched to a trump to East's ace, a trump back from East would be won in dummy and declarer would have the problem of guessing whether to play for diamonds 3–3 or for the ruffing finesse (West having dropped the cost-free ◇Q under the ◇K earlier). With only one trump left in dummy, South would need to take the winning position and while he may pick it correctly, one cannot have the opposition go wrong if one never gives them the chance.

15. LEND ME YOUR EARS

♠ A K 8
♡ K J 2
◇ J 4 2
♣ A 7 6 5

Match-pointed pairs, East–West vulnerable
Dealer East

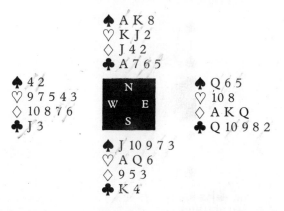

WEST	NORTH	EAST	SOUTH
		1♣	1♠
No bid	4♠	All pass	

♠ J 10 9 7 3
♡ A Q 6
◇ 9 5 3
♣ K 4

1. West led the jack of clubs . . .

HOW SHOULD SOUTH PLAN THE PLAY?

HOW THE PLAY WENT:

                    ♠ A K 8
                    ♡ K J 2
                    ◇ J 4 2
                    ♣ A 7 6 5

♠ 4 2   ♠ Q 6 5
♡ 9 7 5 4 3   ♡ 10 8
◇ 10 8 7 6   ◇ A K Q
♣ J 3   ♣ Q 10 9 8 2

                    ♠ J 10 9 7 3
                    ♡ A Q 6
                    ◇ 9 5 3
                    ♣ K 4

South won the club lead with the king and led the jack of spades, finessing when West played low. East won the queen of spades and cashed three diamonds. One down.

"Nothing I could have done, partner," said South.

WAS SOUTH RIGHT OR WRONG?

Solution:

It is true that if East began with Q–x–x or longer in spades, South was bound to fail, barring a most unlikely and risky elimination play (win ♣K, ♣A and ruff a club, cash three rounds of hearts ending in dummy and ruff dummy's last club and exit with a diamond: if East began with

♠ Q x x   ♡ x x x   ◇ A K Q   ♣ Q x x x

this elimination play would work).

Nevertheless, South played the hand poorly. Firstly, if one is going to take the spade finesse one should cash one top trump honour first. One never knows when one might get lucky and drop a singleton queen. Secondly, the queen of spades was almost certainly marked in the East hand. After the ♣J lead, only 13 points were not visible to declarer. If East did not hold the ♠Q, it meant that East had opened 1♣ on an 11-count at best. Most players would be reluctant to do that without exceptional distribution and you should normally assume that the opening bidder has 12 + points.

The complete hand was:

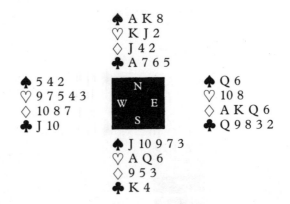

```
                 ♠ A K 8
                 ♡ K J 2
                 ◇ J 4 2
                 ♣ A 7 6 5
  ♠ 5 4 2              N        ♠ Q 6
  ♡ 9 7 5 4 3                   ♡ 10 8
  ◇ 10 8 7        W      E      ◇ A K Q 6
  ♣ J 10               S        ♣ Q 9 8 3 2
                 ♠ J 10 9 7 3
                 ♡ A Q 6
                 ◇ 9 5 3
                 ♣ K 4
```

After winning the ♣K, South should play ace and king of spades, hoping that the queen of trumps falls singleton or doubleton. In practice that play would have succeeded. One could also start the elimination play: win the ♣K, cross to the ♣A and ruff a club high. If West follows to the third club, one could continue with three rounds of hearts and ruff the last club high, followed by the diamond exit. If, however, West discards on the third club (particularly if he discards a heart) you should leave the elimination and play to drop the queen of trumps.

Full marks if you spotted the elimination play and rejected it.

16. A MAJOR CALAMITY

♠ K Q 3
♡ K Q 10 7 2
◇ A J 10
♣ A J

Match points, nil vulnerable
Dealer West

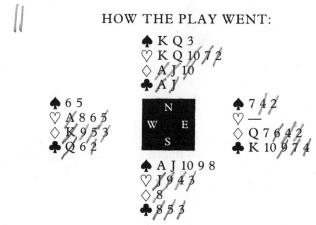

WEST	NORTH	EAST	SOUTH
No bid	1♣(1)	No bid	1♠
No bid	2NT(2)	No bid	3♡
No bid	4♣(3)	No bid	4♡
No bid	No bid	No bid	

♠ A J 10 9 8
♡ J 9 4 3
◇ 8
♣ 8 5 3

(1) Artificial, big club.
(2) Shows 20+ points, balanced shape.
(3) Cue bid, agreeing hearts.

1. West led the three of diamonds . . .

HOW SHOULD SOUTH PLAN THE PLAY

HOW THE PLAY WENT:

♠ K Q 3
♡ K Q 10 7 2
◇ A J 10
♣ A J

♠ 6 5
♡ A 8 6 5
◇ K 9 5 3
♣ Q 6 2

♠ 7 4 2
♡ —
◇ Q 7 6 4 2
♣ K 10 9 7 4

♠ A J 10 9 8
♡ J 9 4 3
◇ 8
♣ 8 5 3

South won the ace of diamonds and, cursing at missing a simple slam, played a heart to his nine. East discarded a diamond and West ducked. The bad break was a minor inconvenience but South led a spade to the king, ruffed a diamond and led a low heart. Had West risen South would have had it easy, but West ducked and the ♡7 won. Dummy's last diamond was ruffed with the ♡J and a second spade was won in dummy. The ♡K dislodged the ace and West switched to a club but South won dummy's ace, drew the last trump and claimed twelve tricks.

WHAT ERRORS, IF ANY, WERE COMMITTED?

Solution:

After the hand was over it was North who was cursing for, although a simple slam had been missed, South's carelessness had resulted in 4♡ going down. This was the complete hand:

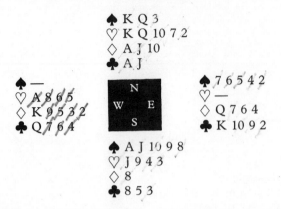

♠ K Q 3
♡ K Q 10 7 2
◇ A J 10
♣ A J

♠ —
♡ A 8 6 5
◇ K 9 5 3 2
♣ Q 7 6 4

♠ 7 6 5 4 2
♡ —
◇ Q 7 6 4
♣ K 10 9 2

♠ A J 10 9 8
♡ J 9 4 3
◇ 8
♣ 8 5 3

South won the ◇A and led a heart to his nine, ducked by West. Now when South led a spade, West ruffed and East gave West a suit-preference signal with the *two* of spades. West naturally found the devastating switch to clubs and nothing South could do could prevent West from gaining the lead with the ♡A, giving East the lead in clubs to receive a second spade ruff and the fourth trick for the defence.

While the spade and heart divisions are very unlucky, South need not have risked anything. At trick two he should have led a diamond from dummy and ruffed high (hardly necessary as East with eight diamonds to the K–Q would have bid, but it costs nothing to ruff high). Next a low heart led to dummy's king. If this is taken by the ace, declarer can claim on gaining the lead. If the ♡K holds and everyone follows, dummy's last diamond is ruffed high and another heart led, claiming.

When East shows out on the first round of hearts, dummy's last diamond is ruffed with the jack of hearts and the low heart led, inserting dummy's seven if West plays low or covering if West plays the eight. Again declarer can claim twelve tricks.

The hand is an object lesson on how easy it is to foul up a simple hand when unexpected bad breaks arise.

17. CAUGHT BY FIRST SLIP

♠ K Q 6 4
♡ Q 10 4
◇ Q 10 6
♣ 8 5 3

Teams, neither side vulnerable
Dealer South

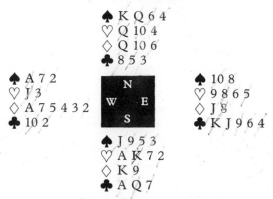

SOUTH	WEST	NORTH	EAST
1NT(1)	No bid	2♣	Double
2♡(2)	No bid	3NT	All pass

♠ J 9 5 3
♡ A K 7 2
◇ K 9
♣ A Q 7

(1) 16–18 points.
(2) Shows four hearts and promises a stopper in clubs. (With no stopper, South would pass allowing North to redouble to find South's answer to Stayman.)

West led the ten of clubs: three–six . . .

HOW SHOULD SOUTH PLAN THE PLAY?

HOW THE PLAY WENT:

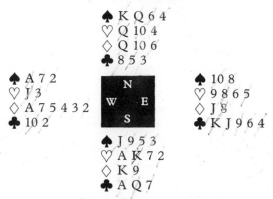

South won the club lead with the queen and led a spade to the king. When that won, a low spade went to the jack and ace. West returned the second club taken by the ace and now declarer cashed the ace of hearts and led a low heart to the jack and queen. The established ten of hearts was cashed followed by the queen of spades and a spade to the nine. The king of hearts was declarer's ninth trick and when he led the king of diamonds, West won but had only diamonds left and had to give declarer an overtrick with the ◇Q.

WHAT ERRORS, IF ANY, WERE COMMITTED?

Solution:
In the bidding North might have bid 3NT directly rather than use Stayman which is rarely profitable on a 4–3–3–3 pattern. Even if a 4–4 fit is discovered, it may still play better in no-trumps as no ruffing value is held and the very use of Stayman is disadvantageous as it gives away some of opener's shape, it allows the opposition to bid cheaply and, as here, it allows a lead directing double of 2♣. For those kind of drawbacks, the price should be right.

On the hand given, East's double on a moderate club collection and no values was adventuresome indeed. Over 3NT, South could have converted to 4♠ since North's sequence expressed interest in a major game.

On the hand given declarer mismanaged the spade suit. After low to the king of spades, he should continue with the queen of spades, catering for the possibility of A–10–x–x with East and retaining the J–9 finessing position.

On the actual hand, declarer in fact failed in 3NT because of an elementary slip. This was the layout:

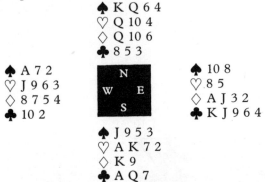

```
              ♠ K Q 6 4
              ♡ Q 10 4
              ◇ Q 10 6
              ♣ 8 5 3
♠ A 7 2                        ♠ 10 8
♡ J 9 6 3          N          ♡ 8 5
◇ 8 7 5 4      W       E      ◇ A J 3 2
♣ 10 2             S          ♣ K J 9 6 4
              ♠ J 9 5 3
              ♡ A K 7 2
              ◇ K 9
              ♣ A Q 7
```

South won the ♣Q at trick one and led a spade. West rose with the ace to lead his second club, taken by the ace. The ace of hearts was followed by a heart to the queen and a third heart, but that suit did not behave. The spades were cashed but East merely discarded his low diamonds and declarer could not come to more than eight tricks before surrendering to East.

South might have made the hand double-dummy by guessing to finesse the ten of hearts or by leading a top diamond before tackling the spades but those are kibitzer-type observations. The main error came from taking the first club. The king of clubs and the club length was marked with East from the bidding and the lead and by holding up at trick one, declarer will succeed if West holds either ace.

Suppose South ducks the first club and West continues clubs. South wins and now tackles spades. When West gains the lead, he is out of clubs and on any switch, South can make overtricks.

18. A SHADE OF MAROON

♠ K 5
♡ 10 7 3 2
♢ J 8
♣ A J 10 9 2

Rubber bridge, East–West vulnerable and +70
Dealer West

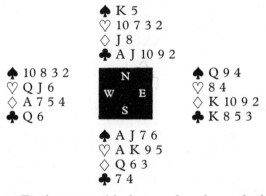

	WEST	NORTH	EAST	SOUTH
	No bid	No bid	No bid	1♡
	No bid	3♡(1)	No bid	4♡(1)
	No bid	No bid	No bid	

♠ A J 7 6
♡ A K 9 5
♢ Q 6 3
♣ 7 4

(1) Anxious to wipe out the East–West part-score.

1. West led the two of spades: five–queen–**ace**.

THANKFUL FOR THE NON-DIAMOND LEAD, HOW SHOULD SOUTH PLAN THE PLAY?

HOW THE PLAY WENT:

♠ K 5
♡ 10 7 3 2
♢ J 8
♣ A J 10 9 2

♠ 10 8 3 2
♡ Q J 6
♢ A 7 5 4
♣ Q 6

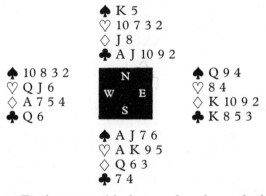

♠ Q 9 4
♡ 8 4
♢ K 10 9 2
♣ K 8 5 3

♠ A J 7 6
♡ A K 9 5
♢ Q 6 3
♣ 7 4

South won East's queen with the ace of spades, cashed one top heart, crossed to the king of spades and returned to hand with a heart to the king, drawing a second round of trumps. Trumps were abandoned and declarer cashed the jack of spades to discard a diamond loser from dummy.

At trick six, declarer led a club to the jack and East's king and East returned the king of diamonds to smother the jack and continued with the ten of diamonds, ruffed in dummy. Declarer played the ace of clubs and when West's queen dropped, declarer claimed stating he would continue clubs till West ruffed at which time dummy would be high.

WHAT ERRORS WERE COMMITTED?

Solution:

When East took the lead, he should have returned a low diamond instead of the king so that if West obtained the lead with the ace, he could draw a third round of trumps. On the layout given, that would not have altered the hand since the ♣Q falls fortuitously on the second round of clubs. In real life, however, declarer went down when the clubs did not fall so prettily even though they were favourably split 3–3 with the honours divided. This was the hand:

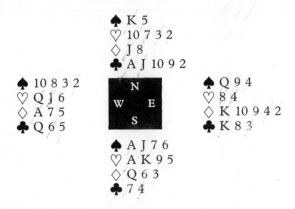

```
                    ♠ K 5
                    ♡ 10 7 3 2
                    ◇ J 8
                    ♣ A J 10 9 2
  ♠ 10 8 3 2            N          ♠ Q 9 4
  ♡ Q J 6                          ♡ 8 4
  ◇ A 7 5          W       E       ◇ K 10 9 4 2
  ♣ Q 6 5                          ♣ K 8 3
                       S
                    ♠ A J 7 6
                    ♡ A K 9 5
                    ◇ Q 6 3
                    ♣ 7 4
```

Declarer failed by following the given line thus:
1. ♠2 led, South winning East's queen with the ace.
2. ♡A cashed.
3. Spade to the king.
4. Heart back to the king.
5. ♠J cashed, discarding one diamond from dummy.
6. Club to the jack and king.
7. East did return a low diamond to West's ace.
8. West cashed the queen of hearts and . . .
9. Returned a diamond . . .

If declarer trumped this, he was marooned in dummy and could not repeat the club finesse (failing when the ♣Q did not drop) while if declarer discarded from dummy, East's ◇K would be the fourth trick for the defence.

Declarer's error was in opening up the heart suit before his preliminary preparations had been completed. The better play is to win the ♣Q with the ace, cross to the ♠K, back to the ace of hearts, cash the ♠J for a diamond discard and then take the club finesse. Now the defence cannot draw a third round of trumps and declarer has an easy time.

19. ANGINA PECTORIS

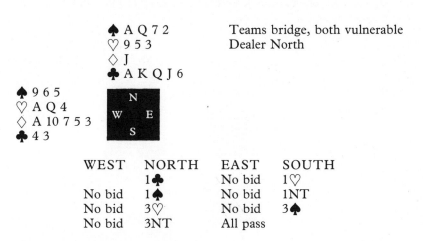

♠ A Q 7 2
♡ 9 5 3
◇ J
♣ A K Q J 6

Teams bridge, both vulnerable
Dealer North

♠ 9 6 5
♡ A Q 4
◇ A 10 7 5 3
♣ 4 3

WEST	NORTH	EAST	SOUTH
	1♣	No bid	1♡
No bid	1♠	No bid	1NT
No bid	3♡	No bid	3♠
No bid	3NT	All pass	

1. West led ◇5: jack–**king**–four.
2. East returned ◇8: queen from South ...

HOW SHOULD WEST PLAN THE DEFENCE?

HOW THE PLAY WENT:

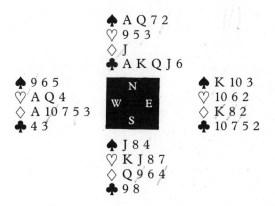

♠ A Q 7 2
♡ 9 5 3
◇ J
♣ A K Q J 6

♠ 9 6 5
♡ A Q 4
◇ A 10 7 5 3
♣ 4 3

♠ K 10 3
♡ 10 6 2
◇ K 8 2
♣ 10 7 5 2

♠ J 8 4
♡ K J 8 7
◇ Q 9 6 4
♣ 9 8

West won the queen of diamonds with the ace and switched to the nine of spades. Declarer played low from dummy and East won the king. East returned the two of diamonds enabling West to take the rest of the diamonds. Down three.

WAS THIS RESULT INEVITABLE? WHAT ERRORS WERE MADE?

Solution:
Declarer in fact made his 3NT contract easily on the given defence. This was the actual hand:

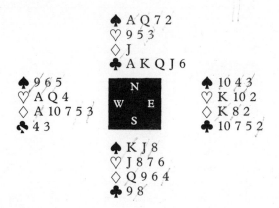

♠ A Q 7 2
♡ 9 5 3
◇ J
♣ A K Q J 6

♠ 9 6 5
♡ A Q 4
◇ A 10 7 5 3
♣ 4 3

N W E S

♠ 10 4 3
♡ K 10 2
◇ K 8 2
♣ 10 7 5 2

♠ K J 8
♡ J 8 7 6
◇ Q 9 6 4
♣ 9 8

When West switched to a spade at trick three, declarer tabled his cards and claimed nine tricks. West excused himself by saying that he expected South to hold the king of hearts for his one heart response and could not tell which major to try.

West's excuse, of course, does not hold water. On the bidding South is marked with three spades, four hearts and a stopper in diamonds. East's return of the eight of diamonds at trick two marks South with Q 9 x x (East would have returned his lowest card if he had started with K 8 x x), and South is known to have the guarded nine of diamonds left. It is therefore correct for West to try to locate his partner's outside entry so that another diamond can be led through.

The proper card for West to lead at trick three, however, is the four of hearts. This caters for East holding either major king. On the above hand East would win with the king of hearts and return his diamond, defeating the contract by four tricks. And if declarer has the heart king no great damage is done. Lacking the king of spades, South cannot score more than five clubs, one heart and one spade before giving the defence the lead again.

ADVANCED LEVEL
DEALS 20 TO 38

20. COUNTERPOINT

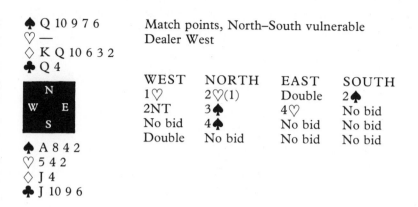

♠ Q 10 9 7 6
♡ —
◇ K Q 10 6 3 2
♣ Q 4

Match points, North–South vulnerable
Dealer West

WEST	NORTH	EAST	SOUTH
1♡	2♡(1)	Double	2♠
2NT	3♠	4♡	No bid
No bid	4♠	No bid	No bid
Double	No bid	No bid	No bid

♠ A 8 4 2
♡ 5 4 2
◇ J 4
♣ J 10 9 6

(1) Michaels Convention, showing spades and a minor suit.

1. West led the **ace** of diamonds: two–five–four.
2. West led the eight of diamonds: three–seven–**jack**.

HOW SHOULD SOUTH CONTINUE THE PLAY?

HOW THE PLAY WENT:

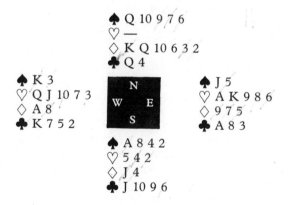

♠ Q 10 9 7 6
♡ —
◇ K Q 10 6 3 2
♣ Q 4

♠ K 3
♡ Q J 10 7 3
◇ A 8
♣ K 7 5 2

♠ J 5
♡ A K 9 8 6
◇ 9 7 5
♣ A 8 3

♠ A 8 4 2
♡ 5 4 2
◇ J 4
♣ J 10 9 6

After winning the jack of diamonds, South continued with ace and another spade. West won the king of spades and promptly switched to clubs. The defence took their two club tricks for one down.

WHAT ERRORS, IF ANY, WERE COMMITTED?

Solution:
By taking the line stated, declarer in fact went two down instead of just one down. At matchpoints, of course, −500 against a non-vulnerable game was a disaster but at no form of the game is it attractive to go −500 when you can logically restrict yourself to −200. This was the actual layout which declarer should have foreseen:

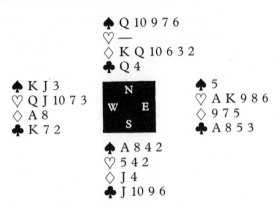

```
                    ♠ Q 10 9 7 6
                    ♡ —
                    ◇ K Q 10 6 3 2
                    ♣ Q 4
    ♠ K J 3                          ♠ 5
    ♡ Q J 10 7 3        N            ♡ A K 9 8 6
    ◇ A 8           W       E        ◇ 9 7 5
    ♣ K 7 2             S            ♣ A 8 5 3
                    ♠ A 8 4 2
                    ♡ 5 4 2
                    ◇ J 4
                    ♣ J 10 9 6
```

After ace and another diamond, when South led ace of spades and another spade, West won the king of spades. Then came the king of clubs, a club to the ace and East played the third diamond, allowing West to make his jack of spades for down two.

West was pretty well marked with the king and jack of spades, firstly because of his willingness to try no-trumps in the face of the North–South spade fit and, secondly, because he persevered with diamonds at trick two, hardly the action of a player holding K-x in trumps. South's correct play at trick three was to lead a low spade towards dummy's queen. Then, if West rises with the king, cashes the king of clubs and leads a club to the ace, South should ruff East's diamond return with the ace of spades. He can then finesse the ten of spades in dummy, holding the contract to one off.

If on the low spade lead towards dummy, West plays low, South's best bet is to rise with dummy's queen. If West did begin with K-J-x-x in spades, declarer now has two trump losers but if the spades are 4–0, declarer cannot prevent West from making two trump tricks if East has an entry in clubs, as is virtually certain.

21. WHAT IS THE RIGHT TIME?

♠ 6 2
♡ K 6 4 2
◇ J 9 6 5 4 2
♣ 9

Teams, North–South vulnerable
Dealer East

	WEST	NORTH	EAST	SOUTH
			2♠(1)	Double (2)
	No bid	3♡	No bid	3NT(2)
	No bid	No bid	No bid	

♠ Q J 7 3
♡ A 10 5
◇ A K 10
♣ A 10 6

(1) Weak two, 6–10 points, six-card suit.
(2) Very aggressive action by South who treated his hand as too strong for an immediate 2NT over 2♠ because of the deep double stopper in spades and all those tens. The final contract is more than reasonable.
West led the king of clubs, East followed with the five.

HOW SHOULD SOUTH PLAN THE PLAY?

HOW THE PLAY WENT:

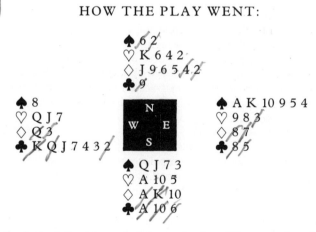

♠ 6 2
♡ K 6 4 2
◇ J 9 6 5 4 2
♣ 9

♠ 8
♡ Q J 7
◇ Q 3
♣ K Q J 7 4 3 2

♠ A K 10 9 5 4
♡ 9 8 3
◇ 8 7
♣ 8 5

♠ Q J 7 3
♡ A 10 5
◇ A K 10
♣ A 10 6

South ducked the king of clubs and when West continued with the queen of clubs, South held up the ace again. South won the third club, cashed the ace and king of diamonds and made nine tricks precisely.

WERE ANY ERRORS MADE AND IF SO, BY WHOM?

53

Solution:
South failed because he held up twice in clubs. If the queen of diamonds falls singleton or doubleton, declarer is always cold for nine tricks and declarer has no option about how to play the diamonds as he cannot afford to use the ♡K as an entry to take the diamond finesse, even if it succeeded.

If the diamonds behave, there are no problems. If West with the long clubs has Q–x–x in diamonds, equally there are no problems as it is just a matter of how many down you will go. However, it is possible that East has the guarded queen of diamonds and in that case the second hold up in clubs is fatal. That is precisely what happened when the hand was played, for this was the layout:

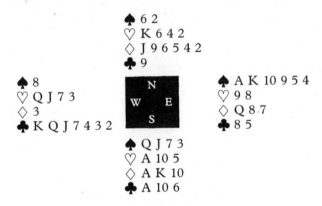

```
                    ♠ 6 2
                    ♡ K 6 4 2
                    ◇ J 9 6 5 4 2
                    ♣ 9
    ♠ 8                              ♠ A K 10 9 5 4
    ♡ Q J 7 3          N             ♡ 9 8
    ◇ 3            W       E         ◇ Q 8 7
    ♣ K Q J 7 4 3 2      S           ♣ 8 5
                    ♠ Q J 7 3
                    ♡ A 10 5
                    ◇ A K 10
                    ♣ A 10 6
```

Declarer ducked two rounds of clubs and won the third. He then cashed ◇ A–K, conceded a diamond to East's queen and was one off when East cleverly cashed his ♠A–K.

South should win the second round of clubs. If East has Q–x–x in diamonds, the only problem position, he is likely to have no more than two clubs and if East were 6–1–3–3, South was never going to make the contract anyway (although he could limit his undertricks).

After winning the ♣A at trick two, South plays ace, king and a third diamond. When East wins and does not return a third club, he is marked with a 6–2–3–2 shape. On a heart return, South can win the ♡K, cash the diamonds and lead a spade or win the ♡A, cross to the ♡K, run the diamonds and lead a spade. He cannot be prevented from setting up a spade for his ninth trick.

22. MARKED CARDS

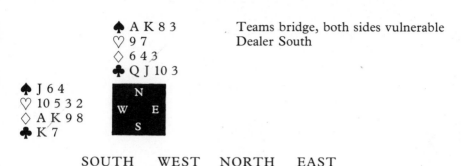

♠ A K 8 3
♡ 9 7
◇ 6 4 3
♣ Q J 10 3

Teams bridge, both sides vulnerable
Dealer South

♠ J 6 4
♡ 10 5 3 2
◇ A K 9 8
♣ K 7

SOUTH	WEST	NORTH	EAST
2♡(1)	No bid	No bid	No bid

(1) Weak two bid, 6–10 points, 6-card suit.

1. West led the king of diamonds: three–ten–two.

HOW SHOULD WEST PLAN THE DEFENCE?

HOW THE PLAY WENT:

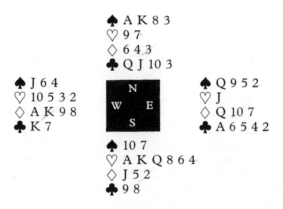

♠ A K 8 3
♡ 9 7
◇ 6 4 3
♣ Q J 10 3

♠ J 6 4
♡ 10 5 3 2
◇ A K 9 8
♣ K 7

♠ Q 9 5 2
♡ J
◇ Q 10 7
♣ A 6 5 4 2

♠ 10 7
♡ A K Q 8 6 4
◇ J 5 2
♣ 9 8

West led the king of diamonds, and in response to East's encouraging ten, continued with the ace of diamonds and a third diamond. East then played ace of clubs and a club to West's king. Declarer could not avoid a trump loser and the defence could not come to more than one trump trick so that the result was one down.

WHAT ERRORS, IF ANY, WERE COMMITTED?

Solution:
The defence found by West allowed declarer to make his contract in comfort when the killing defence could have been found easily with a little logic. This was the actual hand:

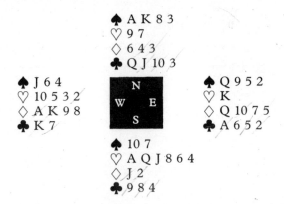

<pre>
              ♠ A K 8 3
              ♡ 9 7
              ◇ 6 4 3
              ♣ Q J 10 3
  ♠ J 6 4   ♠ Q 9 5 2
  ♡ 10 5 3 2   N   ♡ K
  ◇ A K 9 8   W   E   ◇ Q 10 7 5
  ♣ K 7   S   ♣ A 6 5 2
              ♠ 10 7
              ♡ A Q J 8 6 4
              ◇ J 2
              ♣ 9 8 4
</pre>

After ace, king and a third diamond, South was able to ruff, cross to the ace of spades and lead a heart, king, ace. The queen and jack of trumps were cashed and then a club was led. The defence came to two diamonds, two clubs and a trump trick, but that was all so that declarer made his contract.

After the first trick, a little reflection would help West find the best chance of success. East's ten of diamonds denies the jack and as South is marked with six hearts, East can have at most the bare ace of hearts. Thus, South can be placed with at least K–Q–J of hearts and the jack of diamonds. Hence he cannot also have the ace of clubs, for that would give him 11 points and more likely a 1♡ opening rather than a weak 2♡.

Accordingly, West should switch to the king of clubs at trick two. The play then proceeding: ♣K, club to the ace, club ruffed by West. West should then underlead his ace of diamonds to East's queen and the fourth round of clubs will promote West's ten of hearts as the setting trick.

West can expect East to hold the queen of diamonds, not only from a suit-preference signal when East plays the third club but also because if East's ◇10 had been the beginning of a doubleton, East would have played a second diamond after coming in with the ace of clubs. East can also tell to play the fourth round of clubs rather than a third round of diamonds, for if West did not hold a trump that could be promoted, West would have continued with the ace of diamonds instead of leading away from his known ace.

23. SET 'EM UP, JOE

♠ A K Q 9 7
♡ K Q 3
◇ 5 4
♣ K J 10

Rubber bridge, neither side vulnerable
Dealer East

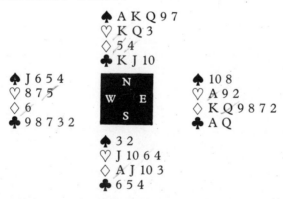

WEST	NORTH	EAST	SOUTH
		1◇	No bid
No bid	Double	No bid	1NT
No bid	3NT	All pass	

♠ 3 2
♡ J 10 6 4
◇ A J 10 3
♣ 6 5 4

1. West led ◇6: four–queen–**ace**.
2. South led ♡6: five–king–**ace**.
3. East returned ◇7: South's jack won and *West discarded ♣3*.

HOW SHOULD SOUTH PLAN THE PLAY FROM HERE?

HOW THE PLAY WENT:

♠ A K Q 9 7
♡ K Q 3
◇ 5 4
♣ K J 10

♠ J 6 5 4   ♠ 10 8
♡ 8 7 5   ♡ A 9 2
◇ 6   ◇ K Q 9 8 7 2
♣ 9 8 7 3 2   ♣ A Q

♠ 3 2
♡ J 10 6 4
◇ A J 10 3
♣ 6 5 4

After winning the ◇J at trick three, South saw the danger of letting West obtain the lead in spades for a club switch from West would then give the defence five tricks if East had ♣A–Q or if South misguesses the club position. Accordingly, South took a safety play in spades and led a low spade to the nine. East won the ten of spades and no matter what he returned, South was in control. In practice, East exited with a heart and declarer had four spades, three hearts and two diamonds for contract.

WHAT ERRORS, IF ANY, WERE COMMITTED AND BY WHOM?

Solution:
Had the layout been as that indicated in the problem, East would have committed a serious error by winning the ace of hearts on the first round. By ducking the ace of hearts, he can cut declarer off from his hand and declarer would have to pull off an endplay on East to succeed. While declarer might succeed, declarer might also fail, for instance by playing four rounds of spades and giving West the lead to push a club through.

However the actual layout was slightly different and declarer failed in practice when he took the "safety" play in spades at trick four. This was the hand:

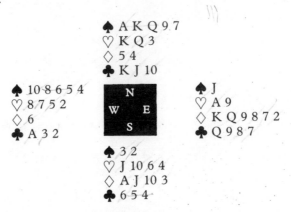

In practice the play went: ◇6 to the queen and ace, heart to the king and ace, ◇7 won by South's jack and a spade went to dummy's nine and East's jack. East exited with the ♡9 won by dummy's queen. Declarer tested the spades and was crestfallen at the bad split. He ran the two heart winners from hand and then led a club, naturally enough mispicking when West played low. East won the ♣Q, cashed the top diamond and led a club to West's ace as the setting trick.

Although declarer was unlucky, he could have made certain of the contract once he had made a second diamond at trick three and still had a diamond stopper. With three spade and three heart winners in addition to the two diamond tricks, declarer need do no more than set up a club winner by force. At trick four he merely leads a club to the jack and continues clubs at each opportunity, unless East perseveres with diamonds and gives South his ninth trick there.

24. IN NO HURRY

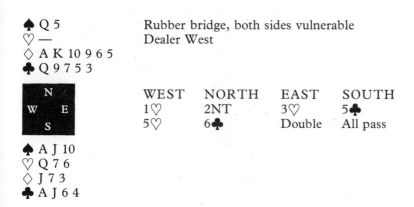

♠ Q 5
♡ —
◇ A K 10 9 6 5
♣ Q 9 7 5 3

Rubber bridge, both sides vulnerable
Dealer West

WEST	NORTH	EAST	SOUTH
1♡	2NT	3♡	5♣
5♡	6♣	Double	All pass

♠ A J 10
♡ Q 7 6
◇ J 7 3
♣ A J 6 4

1. West led ♡K: **three of clubs**–jack of hearts–♡6.
2. ♣Q led from dummy: king–**ace**–*West discarded* ♠*9*.

HOW SHOULD SOUTH PLAN THE PLAY?

HOW THE PLAY WENT:

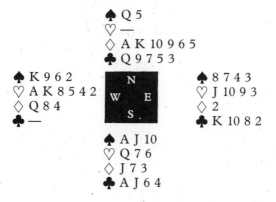

            ♠ Q 5
            ♡ —
            ◇ A K 10 9 6 5
            ♣ Q 9 7 5 3

♠ K 9 6 2   ♠ 8 7 4 3
♡ A K 8 5 4 2   ♡ J 10 9 3
◇ Q 8 4   ◇ 2
♣ —   ♣ K 10 8 2

            ♠ A J 10
            ♡ Q 7 6
            ◇ J 7 3
            ♣ A J 6 4

At trick three, South led a low diamond to dummy's ace, followed by the ♣7. East put in the eight and South ducked. East led a spade but South rose with the ace, ruffed a heart with the ♣9 and led the ♣5, finessing against East's ten. South won the ♣6, drew East's trump with the ♣J and then took the winning position in diamonds, leading the jack and finessing when West played low. Six clubs thus made.

WHAT ERRORS WERE MADE?

59

Solution:
While declarer's line was reasonable, it failed when the diamond break was worse than anticipated:

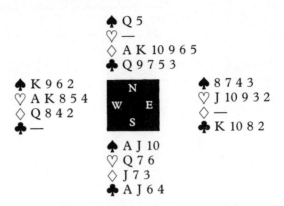

      ♠ Q 5
      ♡ —
      ◇ A K 10 9 6 5
      ♣ Q 9 7 5 3

♠ K 9 6 2   ♠ 8 7 4 3
♡ A K 8 5 4   ♡ J 10 9 3 2
◇ Q 8 4 2   ◇ —
♣ —   ♣ K 10 8 2

      ♠ A J 10
      ♡ Q 7 6
      ◇ J 7 3
      ♣ A J 6 4

 The ♡K lead was ruffed in dummy and the ♣Q, covered by the king, was won by the ace. When declarer led a diamond to the ace, East ruffed and East still had a natural trump trick. One down.

 Once East turns up with all the clubs (and the ♡J), the diamond length and the ◇Q are marked with West, but there is no rush to play the diamonds. At trick three South should lead a low club to dummy's nine. If East ducks, a club to the jack followed by the ◇J, finessing, gives declarer an easy time. If East takes the ♣10 and leads a spade, South rises with the ace, ruffs a heart with the ♣7 and finesses East's remaining trumps, followed by the ◇J, finessing on the first round, of course.

25. THE EARLY BIRD

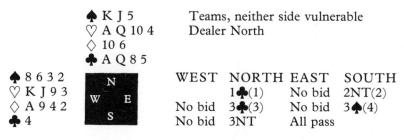

♠ K J 5   Teams, neither side vulnerable
♡ A Q 10 4   Dealer North
◇ 10 6
♣ A Q 8 5

	WEST	NORTH	EAST	SOUTH
		1♣(1)	No bid	2NT(2)
	No bid	3♣(3)	No bid	3♠(4)
	No bid	3NT	All pass	

(1) Precision, 16+ points.
(2) 11–13 points, balanced.
(3) Asking about majors.
(4) Shows four spades, denies four hearts.

1. West led the two of diamonds: six–**king**–three.
2. East returned the jack of diamonds: queen–**ace**–ten.
3. West cashed the **nine** of diamonds: ♡4 discard–◇5–◇8.

DO YOU AGREE WITH THE PLAY SO FAR?

HOW SHOULD WEST CONTINUE?

HOW THE PLAY WENT:

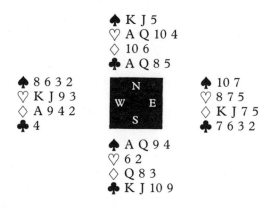

           ♠ K J 5
           ♡ A Q 10 4
           ◇ 10 6
           ♣ A Q 8 5

♠ 8 6 3 2   ♠ 10 7
♡ K J 9 3   ♡ 8 7 5
◇ A 9 4 2   ◇ K J 7 5
♣ 4   ♣ 7 6 3 2

           ♠ A Q 9 4
           ♡ 6 2
           ◇ Q 8 3
           ♣ K J 10 9

At trick four West continued with the fourth round of diamonds. East won with the seven of diamonds. Declarer discarded a heart and tabled his cards, claiming.

HAVE ANY ERRORS BEEN COMMITTED?

Solution:
In actual practice, declarer made his contract when the defence went along the lines given, but the defence could have given declarer a chance to go wrong, a chance that declarer would almost inevitably have taken. This was the complete hand:

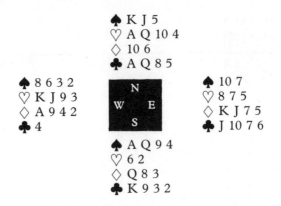

♠ K J 5
♡ A Q 10 4
◇ 10 6
♣ A Q 8 5

♠ 8 6 3 2
♡ K J 9 3
◇ A 9 4 2
♣ 4

♠ 10 7
♡ 8 7 5
◇ K J 7 5
♣ J 10 7 6

♠ A Q 9 4
♡ 6 2
◇ Q 8 3
♣ K 9 3 2

The play went as described: ◇2 to the king; ◇J–Q–A; ◇9 and a diamond to East's seven. East exited with a spade. Declarer won the spade in dummy, cashed the ace and queen of clubs and when the 4–1 break appeared, he took his spade winners and finessed the queen of hearts for his ninth trick. Making 3NT.

West should have been aware of this possibility. With South marked with at least 11 points and East turning up with ◇K–J on the first two tricks, West could tell that South had to have every missing picture except possibly the ♣J. That gave South eight tricks (four spades, three clubs and the ♡A). If South had the ♣J as well, 3NT was unbeatable but if East had that card, South would fall back on the heart finesse unless he had not yet found out about the bad club break.

After cashing the nine of diamonds, West should have led the nine of hearts. On the above hand, South would hardly have risked the heart finesse, but once he has taken the ace of hearts, he must fail. In fact, the best moment for West to lead the nine of hearts is after winning the second diamond, making it appear as though he is trying to put East on lead to play another diamond through South.

The early heart play from West would still be best if South had only K–x–x in clubs. He might then take the heart finesse rather than rely on 3–3 clubs, but if West does not put pressure on South early, South has no option but to succeed later via the heart finesse.

As for the early play, East's jack of diamonds was of course correct but West's ◇9 at trick three could have been bettered.

26. LIE OF THE LAND

♠ A K Q 8 5 3
♡ 10
◇ K 9 4
♣ K Q 6

Rubber bridge, North–South vulnerable
Dealer West

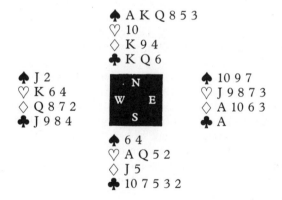

WEST	NORTH	EAST	SOUTH
No bid	1♠	No bid	1NT
No bid	3♠	No bid	3NT
No bid	No bid	No bid	

♠ 6 4
♡ A Q 5 2
◇ J 5
♣ 10 7 5 3 2

1. West led the two of diamonds: four–**ace**–five.
2. East returned the ◇3: jack–**queen**–nine.
3. West continued with ◇8: **king**–six . . .

HOW SHOULD SOUTH CONTINUE THE PLAY?

HOW THE PLAY WENT:

```
              ♠ A K Q 8 5 3
              ♡ 10
              ◇ K 9 4
              ♣ K Q 6
  ♠ J 2              N              ♠ 10 9 7
  ♡ K 6 4       W         E        ♡ J 9 8 7 3
  ◇ Q 8 7 2          S             ◇ A 10 6 3
  ♣ J 9 8 4                        ♣ A
              ♠ 6 4
              ♡ A Q 5 2
              ◇ J 5
              ♣ 10 7 5 3 2
```

South discarded a heart on the king of diamonds and, as the play so far had indicated that diamonds were 4–4, he continued with the king of clubs from dummy. East won the ace, cashed the ten of diamonds, South throwing a heart and dummy throwing the six of clubs, and then led a heart. South refused the heart finesse, stepping up with the ace and with six spades, a heart, a diamond and a club, South had his game contract.

WHAT ERRORS, IF ANY, WERE COMMITTED?

Solution:
South might have passed 3♠ or raised to 4♠ but 3NT is certainly a reasonable spot. We have all been in worse games. Declarer did take the right inference from the early play that diamonds were 4–4 but he nevertheless failed in 3NT when he took the stated line, while he might have succeeded as the cards lay, had he taken a slight precaution. This was the actual hand:

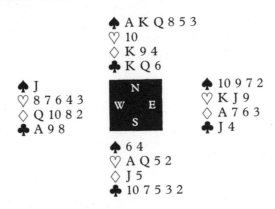

While a heart lead might have made things awkward, West in fact led his stronger suit. East won and returned a diamond and the ◇K took trick three. While it was reasonable to set up a club trick, there was no urgency about it. The correct play is to tackle the spades first. If spades are 3–2, declarer can take his six spade tricks and later elect whether to try for the heart finesse or more likely, set up a club winner.

When spades are found to be 4–1, it is pointless to give up a spade trick since that gives the defence five tricks. South has to start praying for miracles and should take his top three spades and then play the king of clubs. If that holds, continue with the queen of clubs. Declarer has to hope that the ♣J will fall doubleton, that the ♣A and the high diamond are both in the hand which does not hold the established spade winner. It is a lot to expect but nothing less will do.

27. PLAYING UP

♠ 7 6 5
♡ K 9 6 4 2
◇ K 8 3
♣ A 4

Teams bridge, North–South vulnerable
Dealer South

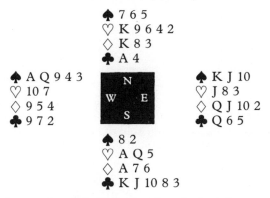

SOUTH	WEST	NORTH	EAST
1NT(1)	No bid	2◇(2)	No bid
2♡	No bid	3NT	No bid
4♡	No bid	No bid	No bid

♠ 8 2
♡ A Q 5
◇ A 7 6
♣ K J 10 8 3

(1) 14–15 points.
(2) Transfer to hearts.

1. West led the seven of clubs: four–queen–**king**.

HOW SHOULD SOUTH CONTINUE?

HOW THE PLAY WENT:

        ♠ 7 6 5
        ♡ K 9 6 4 2
        ◇ K 8 3
        ♣ A 4

♠ A Q 9 4 3   ♠ K J 10
♡ 10 7   ♡ J 8 3
◇ 9 5 4   ◇ Q J 10 2
♣ 9 7 2   ♣ Q 6 5

        ♠ 8 2
        ♡ A Q 5
        ◇ A 7 6
        ♣ K J 10 8 3

As South won the ♣Q with the king, he jovially remarked, "Might have missed six here, partner."

Ace of hearts, queen of hearts and a heart to the king picked up the trumps. The ace of clubs was unblocked and a diamond to the ace saw South taking three club winners to discard dummy's spades.

Conceding just a diamond, South jestingly told North, "Bid up, partner."

WHAT ERRORS, IF ANY, WERE COMMITTED?

Solution:
After following the play outlined, declarer in fact failed in his contract. After the hand was over, North not so jestingly told South, "Play up, partner." This is the layout that provoked North.

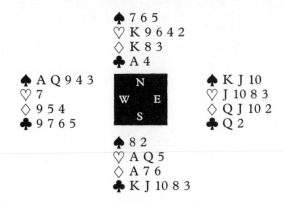

♠ 7 6 5
♡ K 9 6 4 2
◇ K 8 3
♣ A 4

♠ A Q 9 4 3
♡ 7
◇ 9 5 4
♣ 9 7 6 5

♠ K J 10
♡ J 10 8 3
◇ Q J 10 2
♣ Q 2

♠ 8 2
♡ A Q 5
◇ A 7 6
♣ K J 10 8 3

After the club lead ducked to the queen and king, South cashed the A–Q of hearts, receiving the bad news. Next the ♣A was cashed and a diamond played to South's ace. On the ♣J, a diamond was discarded from dummy but East ruffed this and returned his last trump stranding declarer in dummy with three more unavoidable losers. One down.

Particularly when a contract looks dead easy must the greatest caution be exercised. Bitter experience teaches that when all looks rosy, bad breaks are just around the corner. Declarer can take a simple precaution against the not-so-unusual breaks in hearts and clubs.

After winning the ♣K, declarer cashes the ace of hearts but should then play a heart to the king as the second round of hearts. If hearts are 3–2, the last trump is drawn and the rest is easy. When the bad split is known, the ♣A is cashed, a heart is returned to the queen, *thus preserving the ace of diamonds for an entry later*. On the jack of clubs, a spade is discarded from dummy and whether East ruffs now or later, declarer makes his contract in comfort.

28. THE UPSHOT

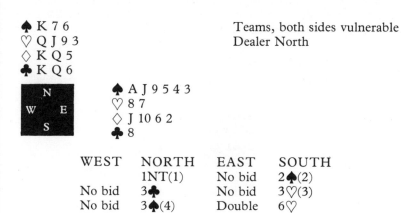

♠ K 7 6
♡ Q J 9 3
◇ K Q 5
♣ K Q 6

Teams, both sides vulnerable
Dealer North

♠ A J 9 5 4 3
♡ 8 7
◇ J 10 6 2
♣ 8

WEST	NORTH	EAST	SOUTH
	1NT(1)	No bid	2♠(2)
No bid	3♣	No bid	3♡(3)
No bid	3♠(4)	Double	6♡

(1) 15–18 points.
(2) Transfer to clubs.
(3) Natural, second suit.
(4) Support for hearts but preference for no-trumps.

1. West led the ♠2: six . . .

HOW SHOULD EAST PLAN THE DEFENCE?

HOW THE PLAY WENT:

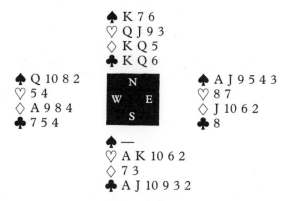

♠ K 7 6
♡ Q J 9 3
◇ K Q 5
♣ K Q 6

♠ Q 10 8 2
♡ 5 4
◇ A 9 8 4
♣ 7 5 4

♠ A J 9 5 4 3
♡ 8 7
◇ J 10 6 2
♣ 8

♠ —
♡ A K 10 6 2
◇ 7 3
♣ A J 10 9 3 2

   East inserted the jack of spades, ruffed by South. Trumps were cleared in two rounds and then six rounds of clubs allowed dummy's diamonds to be discarded. The rest of the hand was crossruffed for thirteen tricks.

ANYTHING WRONG?

Solution:

In practice, East rose with the ace of spades on the lead. Assuming South followed to that spade with the queen, how should East continue?

When the hand arose in the final of a teams event, East would have allowed an impossible slam to make had he played the jack on the first round of spades. The actual hand was:

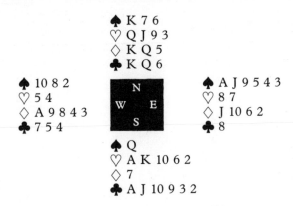

♠ K 7 6
♡ Q J 9 3
◇ K Q 5
♣ K Q 6

♠ 10 8 2
♡ 5 4
◇ A 9 8 4 3
♣ 7 5 4

♠ A J 9 5 4 3
♡ 8 7
◇ J 10 6 2
♣ 8

♠ Q
♡ A K 10 6 2
◇ 7
♣ A J 10 9 3 2

At the table East rose with the ace of spades and returned a diamond for one off. At the other table, North–South used Blackwood and stopped in 5♡.

Finding the ♠A at trick one is not too tough. The worst that could happen is that you stick the ace into South's void but looking at dummy and recalling the bidding, it is clear that South cannot have a crucial discard on the thus established king of spades. Again, once the ace of spades holds, the diamond switch is marked. Any loser in clubs or hearts cannot disappear but a diamond loser may disappear on the king of spades.

There was some suggestion that West ought to lead the eight of spades and not the two in this situation. While that would work on the given hand, it is easy to see that such a practice could give East headaches on a different layout, for example K–x–x in dummy and A–Q–x–x–x–x or A–Q–J–x–x–x with East.

29. THE TELL-TALE HEART

♠ K 8 7 4
♡ K J 5 4
◇ 8
♣ J 10 6 5

Teams, East–West vulnerable
Dealer South

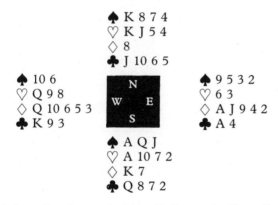

SOUTH	WEST	NORTH	EAST
1NT	No bid	2♣	No bid
2♡	No bid	4♡	All pass

♠ A Q J
♡ A 10 7 2
◇ K 7
♣ Q 8 7 2

1. West led the five of diamonds: eight–**ace**–seven.
2. East switched to the four of clubs: two–**king**–five.
3. West returned the nine of clubs: six–**ace**–queen.
4. East led the four of diamonds . . .

HOW SHOULD SOUTH PLAN THE PLAY?

HOW THE PLAY WENT:

```
              ♠ K 8 7 4
              ♡ K J 5 4
              ◇ 8
              ♣ J 10 6 5
♠ 10 6                        ♠ 9 5 3 2
♡ Q 9 8          N            ♡ 6 3
◇ Q 10 6 5 3   W   E          ◇ A J 9 4 2
♣ K 9 3          S            ♣ A 4
              ♠ A Q J
              ♡ A 10 7 2
              ◇ K 7
              ♣ Q 8 7 2
```

At trick four, South won the king of diamonds, discarding a club from dummy. Then:

5. Two of hearts led: eight–**king**–three.
6. Four of hearts from dummy: six–ten–**queen**.
One down.

WHAT MISTAKES, IF ANY, WERE MADE?

Solution:
On the hand as given, East erred with his switch to a low club at trick two. With little prospect to set the contract without a ruff in clubs, East should have switched to ace and another club. This would have worked instantly on that hand and would also have led to declarer's defeat if West held the ♡A instead of the ♣K and ♡Q.

Declarer took the inference from East's play of a low club from A–x, that East was looking for only two club tricks and hence expected to make a trump trick. That is why declarer placed East with the queen and took the trump finesse through East instead of West. On the actual hand, the queen of hearts was with East (the inference was correct) but declarer still failed on the line taken. What happened?

This was the complete deal:

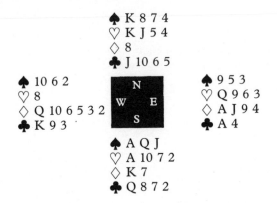

```
              ♠ K 8 7 4
              ♡ K J 5 4
              ◇ 8
              ♣ J 10 6 5
  ♠ 10 6 2                    ♠ 9 5 3
  ♡ 8              N          ♡ Q 9 6 3
  ◇ Q 10 6 5 3 2  W   E      ◇ A J 9 4
  ♣ K 9 3            S        ♣ A 4
              ♠ A Q J
              ♡ A 10 7 2
              ◇ K 7
              ♣ Q 8 7 2
```

In the play of the trumps, low to the king and the four back to South's ten saw the ten winning, but East's Q–9 left meant a trump trick for the defence. Declarer's correct play was ♡2 to the king and, West having dropped the eight, then the ♡J from dummy: if East plays low, the jack is run, followed by a finesse of the ten, while if East covers, dummy is entered with the ♠K to finesse against East's 9–6.

Even if the club play by East suggesting possession of the ♡Q had not taken place, it would normally be correct to play the hearts by leading low to the king first and if West produces the eight or nine, to lead the jack next. This covers, in addition to the 3–2 holdings, those positions where East has Q–9–x–x or Q–8–x–x.

30. GRAND DOWNFALL

♠ A K 10 7 6
♡ —
◇ K Q 9 8 3
♣ K 7 5

Rubber bridge. Neither side vulnerable
Dealer North

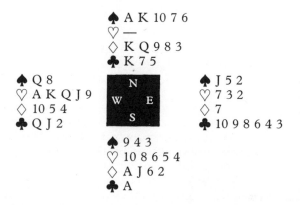

SOUTH	WEST	NORTH	EAST
No bid	1♡	Double	No bid
3◇	3♡	4♡	No bid
5♣	No bid	5◇	No bid
5NT	No bid	7◇	All pass

♠ 9 4 3
♡ 10 8 6 5 4
◇ A J 6 2
♣ A

1. West led the four of diamonds . . .

HOW SHOULD SOUTH PLAN THE PLAY?

HOW THE PLAY WENT:

```
                 ♠ A K 10 7 6
                 ♡ —
                 ◇ K Q 9 8 3
                 ♣ K 7 5
   ♠ Q 8               N          ♠ J 5 2
   ♡ A K Q J 9      W     E       ♡ 7 3 2
   ◇ 10 5 4            S          ◇ 7
   ♣ Q J 2                        ♣ 10 9 8 6 4 3
                 ♠ 9 4 3
                 ♡ 10 8 6 5 4
                 ◇ A J 6 2
                 ♣ A
```

Declarer let the ◇4 lead run to his hand, winning East's seven with his ace. The ace of clubs was cashed, the ◇2 led to dummy's king and the ♣K cashed to discard a spade. Dummy's third club was ruffed with the ◇6 followed by the ace and king of spades. When spades were 3–2, declarer was able to trump the third round of spades with the jack of diamonds, ruff a heart to dummy and draw the last trump, claiming.

WERE THERE ANY ERRORS MADE?

Solution:
Declarer in fact failed in his grand slam when he neglected to take two simple precautions. The first is the obvious move of inserting the eight or nine of diamonds at trick one. This, in practice, would hold the trick and declarer would have two high trumps left in hand to take the two ruffs required. From the bidding, West is much more likely to hold six hearts than five and when he turns up with three diamonds by trick three, he is known to have very few black cards.

The line taken failed when the actual layout was like this:

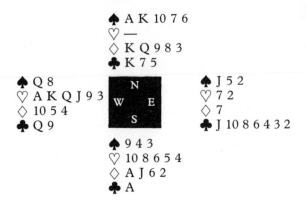

```
              ♠ A K 10 7 6
              ♡ —
              ◇ K Q 9 8 3
              ♣ K 7 5
♠ Q 8                           ♠ J 5 2
♡ A K Q J 9 3      N            ♡ 7 2
◇ 10 5 4        W     E         ◇ 7
♣ Q 9             S            ♣ J 10 8 6 4 3 2
              ♠ 9 4 3
              ♡ 10 8 6 5 4
              ◇ A J 6 2
              ♣ A
```

If South fails to insert the eight or nine of diamonds at trick one, West will be able to overruff South in one of the black suits. Even when the ◇8 wins the first trick, declarer has to proceed carefully. The ♣A wins trick two and the ◇6 is led to dummy's king.

When West turns up with the third diamond and shortages in the black suits, declarer has to assume the spades are 3–2 and West is 2–2 in spades-clubs (South would fail on any other division). The ♣K can be cashed at trick four but declarer must then cash the ace and king of spades before ruffing the third round of clubs. If declarer plays the third club first, West discards a spade and now will be able to ruff the second round of spades.

It appears that it is dangerous to insert the eight or nine of diamonds from dummy, since if West held ◇7 5 4 and East the bare ten, South would again be faced with the danger of being overruffed in one of the black suits. However, it is not safer to win the first trick with the ◇K, cash the ♣A and lead a low diamond to dummy's queen. If it happened that West had started with the singleton diamond and East with ◇10–7–4, this line would now promote a trump trick for East.

31. THE KNOCKOUT

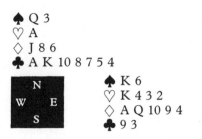

♠ Q 3
♡ A
◇ J 8 6
♣ A K 10 8 7 5 4

♠ K 6
♡ K 4 3 2
◇ A Q 10 9 4
♣ 9 3

Teams, neither side vulnerable
Dealer South

SOUTH	WEST	NORTH	EAST
Pass	Pass	1♣	1◇
1♡	Pass	3♣	Pass
3NT	Pass	Pass	Pass

1. West led the seven of diamonds, eight from dummy . . .

HOW SHOULD EAST PLAN THE DEFENCE?

HOW THE PLAY WENT:

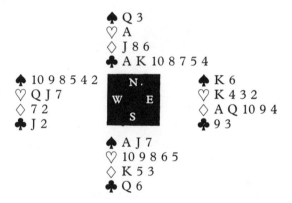

♠ Q 3
♡ A
◇ J 8 6
♣ A K 10 8 7 5 4

♠ 10 9 8 5 4 2
♡ Q J 7
◇ 7 2
♣ J 2

♠ K 6
♡ K 4 3 2
◇ A Q 10 9 4
♣ 9 3

♠ A J 7
♡ 10 9 8 6 5
◇ K 5 3
♣ Q 6

West led the ◇7, the ◇8 from dummy was covered by the nine and South won ◇K. South then ran seven rounds of clubs, discarding four hearts and a diamond. East echoed in hearts and discarded three diamonds while West pitched three spades, one heart and one diamond. Declarer cashed the ace of hearts to make sure of his contract and then led the queen of spades. East covered and South made eleven tricks.

WHAT MISTAKES, IF ANY, WERE MADE AND WHO MADE THEM?

Solution:
East erred in defence by playing the nine of diamonds instead of the ace.

The nine of diamonds is the normal play to set up the diamond suit but the presence of the powerful club suit in dummy indicated that the defence may not have the time to set up and enjoy the diamonds before declarer has his nine tricks.

If declarer has two or more clubs, ducking the first diamond guarantees that South will succeed since he must come to the ◇K, the ♡A and seven clubs. East should win the first trick with the ◇A and then has to choose between two alternative defences: he may switch to the king of spades, hoping to take five or more tricks in spades if West started with AJ10xx, AJxxxx or Axxxxxx OR he may switch to a low heart to knock out the entry to dummy's clubs in case South has only a singleton club.

WHICH IS THE BETTER PLAN?

The actual hand was:

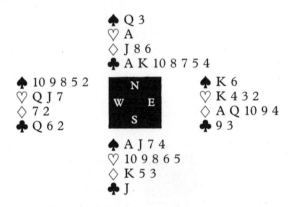

```
                    ♠ Q 3
                    ♡ A
                    ◇ J 8 6
                    ♣ A K 10 8 7 5 4
♠ 10 9 8 5 2                          ♠ K 6
♡ Q J 7              N                ♡ K 4 3 2
◇ 7 2           W        E            ◇ A Q 10 9 4
♣ Q 6 2             S                 ♣ 9 3
                    ♠ A J 7 4
                    ♡ 10 9 8 6 5
                    ◇ K 5 3
                    ♣ J
```

In actual play, East did insert the ◇9 at trick one, South winning the king. South ran the jack of clubs, crossed to the ace of hearts and ultimately made thirteen tricks when West let go spades to hold the hearts.

The killing defence is to win the ◇A and switch to a low heart, thus cutting declarer off from all but the top two clubs. This defence will succeed if South began with ♣J or ♣Q singleton (and also with a rag singleton if West started with only one diamond). After the heart switch, South would almost certainly play ♣ A–K hoping to drop the ♣Q doubleton and when it fails to drop, the contract is several light with good defence.

After the ◇A, East should prefer the heart play rather than the ♠K. If West had a strong spade holding, he may well have bid it over 1♡ or have opened 3♠ with a very long holding.

32. NO RECALL

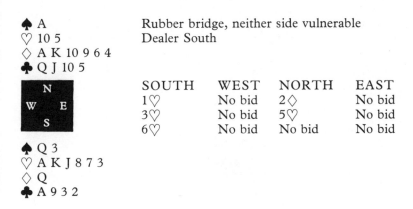

♠ A
♡ 10 5
◇ A K 10 9 6 4
♣ Q J 10 5

Rubber bridge, neither side vulnerable
Dealer South

SOUTH	WEST	NORTH	EAST
1♡	No bid	2◇	No bid
3♡	No bid	5♡	No bid
6♡	No bid	No bid	No bid

♠ Q 3
♡ A K J 8 7 3
◇ Q
♣ A 9 3 2

1. West led the two of hearts: five–nine–**jack**.

HOW SHOULD SOUTH PLAN THE PLAY?

HOW THE PLAY WENT:

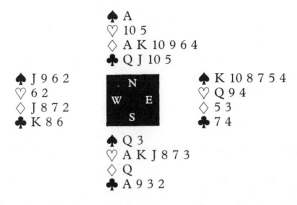

♠ A
♡ 10 5
◇ A K 10 9 6 4
♣ Q J 10 5

♠ J 9 6 2
♡ 6 2
◇ J 8 7 2
♣ K 8 6

♠ K 10 8 7 5 4
♡ Q 9 4
◇ 5 3
♣ 7 4

♠ Q 3
♡ A K J 8 7 3
◇ Q
♣ A 9 3 2

South continued by drawing trumps with the ace and king of hearts, followed by the queen of diamonds. A spade to the ace allowed two top diamonds to be cashed on which a spade and a club were discarded. When the jack of diamonds did not fall, declarer took the club finesse, claiming just twelve tricks when that lost.

WHAT ERRORS WERE COMMITTED?

Solution:

Six clubs is a superior slam but most players would rebid 3♡ on the South cards rather than 3♣.

On the actual hand declarer failed in his slam when he hastily cashed the top trumps at tricks two and three. This was the layout:

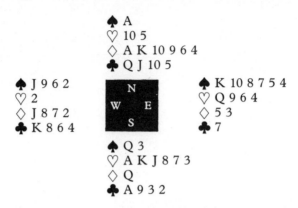

```
                    ♠ A
                    ♡ 10 5
                    ◇ A K 10 9 6 4
                    ♣ Q J 10 5
    ♠ J 9 6 2                        ♠ K 10 8 7 5 4
    ♡ 2          N                   ♡ Q 9 6 4
    ◇ J 8 7 2   W   E                ◇ 5 3
    ♣ K 8 6 4     S                  ♣ 7
                    ♠ Q 3
                    ♡ A K J 8 7 3
                    ◇ Q
                    ♣ A 9 3 2
```

After the ♡2 lead, five, nine, jack, declarer could no longer recover when he cashed the ace of hearts. He won the ◇Q, crossed to the ♠A and took two discards on the two top diamonds (East of course not ruffing the third round). When the club finesse lost South was one down for there was no way to pick up East's queen of hearts.

West's lead was very poor. A singleton trump lead is rarely attractive and there was nothing about the bidding or West's hand to suggest the trump lead. West was wrong to infer from North's 5♡ request for good trumps that the trump suit was solid. The singleton trump lead might just as easily have picked off J–x–x–x in East's hand. Even if the trump were not singleton it was not an attractive start. From the bidding a spade or club lead was indicated and from West's hand the club lead was the more attractive. On a club lead, fearing a ruff and hoping the diamonds might come in, declarer might well lay down the ace-king of trumps with unhappy results.

Declarer's play was very weak. While it was unlikely that West would lead a singleton trump, one thing was sure and that was that West would not have led a trump from Q–x–x. Thus the winning play was to cash the ◇Q, cross to ♠A, cash the ◇K for the spade discard and then lead the ♡10 and run it if East plays low. A diamond ruff to hand, trumps drawn and a club conceded lands the slam. South could even survive easily if East ruffed the second diamond from dummy.

33. DUCK SOUP

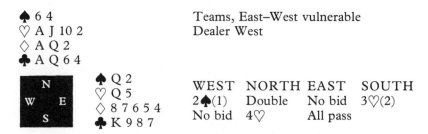

♠ 6 4
♡ A J 10 2
◇ A Q 2
♣ A Q 6 4

Teams, East–West vulnerable
Dealer West

♠ Q 2
♡ Q 5
◇ 8 7 6 5 4
♣ K 9 8 7

WEST	NORTH	EAST	SOUTH
2♠(1)	Double	No bid	3♡(2)
No bid	4♡	All pass	

(1) Weak, 6–10 points, 6-card suit.
(2) Shows a heart suit and reasonable high card values. North–South play an extension of the Lebensohl convention whereby over a double of a weak two, 2NT would require the doubler to bid 3♣ (on a normal double). 2NT followed by 3♡ over the forced 3♣ reply would have shown a heart suit with very weak values.

1. West led the jack of clubs: **ace**–nine–three.
2. **Ace** of hearts from dummy: five–three–seven.
3. Jack of hearts: queen–four–**king**.
4. West continued with the two of clubs, four from dummy . . .

HOW SHOULD EAST PLAN THE DEFENCE?

HOW THE PLAY WENT:

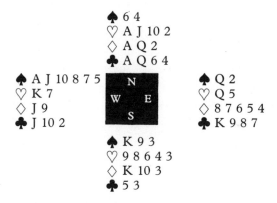

♠ 6 4
♡ A J 10 2
◇ A Q 2
♣ A Q 6 4

♠ A J 10 8 7 5
♡ K 7
◇ J 9
♣ J 10 2

♠ Q 2
♡ Q 5
◇ 8 7 6 5 4
♣ K 9 8 7

♠ K 9 3
♡ 9 8 6 4 3
◇ K 10 3
♣ 5 3

At trick four, East won with the seven of clubs.
East then switched to the queen of spades, king, ace and the jack of spades defeated declarer by one trick.

WHAT MISTAKES, IF ANY, WERE MADE?

Solution:
When the hand arose at the table, East's defence allowed declarer to make his contract. This was the actual hand:

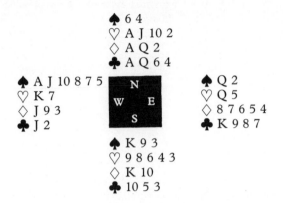

♠ 6 4
♥ A J 10 2
♦ A Q 2
♣ A Q 6 4

♠ A J 10 8 7 5   ♠ Q 2
♥ K 7   ♥ Q 5
♦ J 9 3   ♦ 8 7 6 5 4
♣ J 2   ♣ K 9 8 7

♠ K 9 3
♥ 9 8 6 4 3
♦ K 10
♣ 10 5 3

With no attractive choice, West led the jack of clubs. Declarer, fearing this to be a singleton, rose with the ♣A and played the ace of hearts and when no honour dropped, continued with the jack of hearts. West persevered with the two of clubs, four from dummy and when East played low, the hand was over. South won the ♣10, discarded his other club on the third diamond and gave up two spades. Making 4♥.

To defeat the contract, East must win the ♣K on the second round of clubs and switch to spades at once. Although the initial lead suggested that West held J–10 or J–10–x in clubs (as J–x is a poor lead), West's continuation of the ♣2 should have dispelled that possibility. With J–10–2 West should have continued with the ten of clubs, not the two, especially in view of East's nine of clubs at trick one. (From J–10–x–x initially, West's normal lead is his fourth-highest.)

When East does switch to spades, it should be the two, not the queen. The defence is seeking no more than two spade tricks and there is a faint possibility that South holds K–J–3 and West A–10–9–8–7–5. South has to pick whether to play the king or the jack if East leads the two and while declarer may get it right, you must at least put him to the test.

Declarer might have made things tougher for East also. After the ace of hearts, a low club from dummy puts a lot of pressure on East to find the right play. If East ducks, South wins the ten and the other club again disappears on the third diamond, quickly followed by a second round of trumps.

34. IN THE LAND OF THE BLIND

♠ A 7 6
♡ A K J 6 5 4
◇ —
♣ K 6 5 4

Rubber bridge, neither side vulnerable
Dealer North

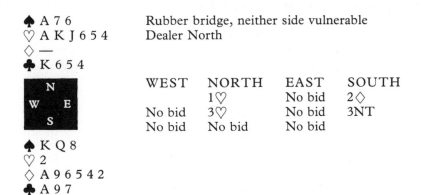

WEST	NORTH	EAST	SOUTH
	1♡	No bid	2◇
No bid	3♡	No bid	3NT
No bid	No bid	No bid	

♠ K Q 8
♡ 2
◇ A 9 6 5 4 2
♣ A 9 7

1. West led the two of clubs: four–queen . . .

HOW SHOULD SOUTH PLAN THE PLAY?

HOW THE PLAY WENT:

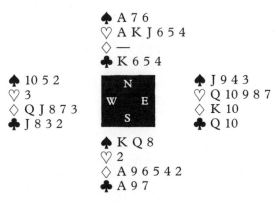

♠ A 7 6
♡ A K J 6 5 4
◇ —
♣ K 6 5 4

♠ 10 5 2
♡ 3
◇ Q J 8 7 3
♣ J 8 3 2

♠ J 9 4 3
♡ Q 10 9 8 7
◇ K 10
♣ Q 10

♠ K Q 8
♡ 2
◇ A 9 6 5 4 2
♣ A 9 7

South won the ♣Q with the ace and hoping either for the ♡Q onside or a favourable break in hearts, led the ♡2 to the jack. East won the queen and naturally enough returned the ten of clubs, taken by the king. Now declarer was all right even if hearts were 4–2 but the ♡A revealed the evil split.

Declarer proceeded by cashing three rounds of spades, ending in hand, and then played ace of diamonds and another diamond. East won the ◇K, cashed the thirteenth spade but had to give dummy an extra heart trick which was the ninth trick for declarer. 3NT made.

HOW MANY MISTAKES WERE MADE AND WHO MADE THEM?

Solution:

On the given layout, East of course should have dropped the king of diamonds under the ace. It was obvious to East that he would be endplayed if he retained the king by a simple count of declarer's tricks. If South held the ◇Q as well as the ace, the contract was unbeatable.

Most defenders would rid themselves of the king of diamonds and in practice declarer failed in 3NT by playing the adopted line. How could declarer have played differently and improved his chance of success?

The genuine chance of success of declarer's line (East holding ◇K–Q or ◇K–Q–J and only three spades) is quite remote. In fact East did hold K–Q bare in diamonds but declarer still failed for this was the hand:

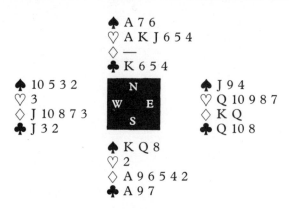

                    ♠ A 7 6
                    ♡ A K J 6 5 4
                    ◇ —
                    ♣ K 6 5 4

    ♠ 10 5 3 2   N   ♠ J 9 4
    ♡ 3   W   E   ♡ Q 10 9 8 7
    ◇ J 10 8 7 3   S   ◇ K Q
    ♣ J 3 2   ♣ Q 10 8

                    ♠ K Q 8
                    ♡ 2
                    ◇ A 9 6 5 4 2
                    ♣ A 9 7

After being 'endplayed' in diamonds, East exited with a third club and West won the ♣J, a spade and his remaining diamonds for down two. After the ace of hearts has revealed that there is little future in hearts, declarer should play a third round of clubs. When clubs are 3–3, declarer has his nine tricks.

Certainly the chance of a 3–3 club break is better than finding East with a precise diamond holding. There is a tendency to have a blind spot when the *two* of clubs is led that clubs are not breaking. Imagine how the play would go on a spade lead: win ♠K, finesse ♡J, win spade return with the ace, cash ♡A, abandon hearts and duck a club etc.

Further, even if clubs are 4–2 the diamond endplay to force East to lead a heart into the K–J has not been lost.

It is also interesting to note that despite the bad break, 4♡ makes very easily.

35. RUN FOR YOUR LIFE

♠ K 5 4
♡ Q 9 6 5
◇ 7
♣ A K Q 10 7

Teams, neither side vulnerable
Dealer North

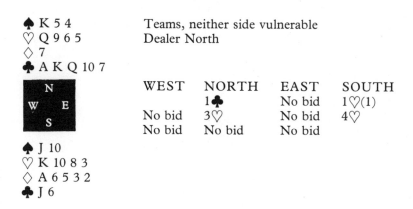

WEST	NORTH	EAST	SOUTH
	1♣	No bid	1♡(1)
No bid	3♡	No bid	4♡
No bid	No bid	No bid	

♠ J 10
♡ K 10 8 3
◇ A 6 5 3 2
♣ J 6

(1) A systemic requirement as opposed to the 1 ◇ response.

1. West led the three of spades: four–eight–**jack**.
2. South played the three of hearts: four–**queen**–two.

HOW SHOULD SOUTH PROCEED WITH THE PLAY?

HOW THE PLAY WENT:

♠ K 5 4
♡ Q 9 6 5
◇ 7
♣ A K Q 10 7

♠ Q 7 6 3 2
♡ A 7 4
◇ K 10 8
♣ 5 4

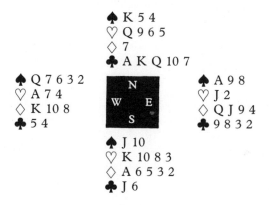

♠ A 9 8
♡ J 2
◇ Q J 9 4
♣ 9 8 3 2

♠ J 10
♡ K 10 8 3
◇ A 6 5 3 2
♣ J 6

After the queen of hearts held, declarer led a second heart and covered East's jack with the king. West won the ace and played the queen of spades and another spade when declarer ducked, but South merely ruffed East's ace, drew the last trump and claimed his contract.

WERE THERE ANY ERRORS COMMITTED?

Solution:

At the table, declarer failed when he played in the way stated. He was the victim of an unfortunate break in trumps but he could have overcome that because of the slice of luck he received. This was the hand:

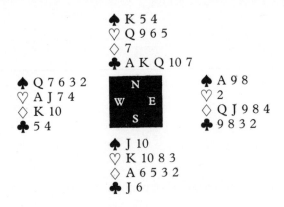

```
              ♠ K 5 4
              ♡ Q 9 6 5
              ◇ 7
              ♣ A K Q 10 7
♠ Q 7 6 3 2        N        ♠ A 9 8
♡ A J 7 4     W       E     ♡ 2
◇ K 10             S        ◇ Q J 9 8 4
♣ 5 4                       ♣ 9 8 3 2
              ♠ J 10
              ♡ K 10 8 3
              ◇ A 6 5 3 2
              ♣ J 6
```

When a low heart to the queen held, it was an error to play a second trump. West won this as East signalled with the four of diamonds, so that West found the killing continuation of the queen of spades. Whatever declarer did, he was forced to trump the next spade. Now, West won the third round of trumps and with West and dummy holding one trump each West led a fourth round of spades. When dummy trumped, declarer had to go three down! West trumped the third round of clubs, cashed his good spade and exited with a diamond to set up a diamond winner as well.

Declarer should have divined what was happening in the spade suit after he was allowed to win the first trick with the jack. Having successfully led a trump to his queen, he should then have abandoned trumps. Instead he should play the jack of clubs and continue with clubs. On the third club, South discards the ten of spades and the defence cannot take more than three trump tricks. Provided the clubs are not 6–0 or 5–1, this line cannot fail.

Declarer's fortunate break came when East ducked the spade lead. This allowed declarer to find the best line. Had East won the ♠A and returned a spade (East could foresee the danger of discards on the clubs), declarer would have had an almost impossible task unless he picked up West's jack of hearts.

36. LET ME OUT OF HERE

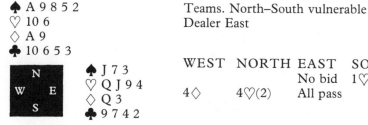

♠ A 9 8 5 2
♡ 10 6
◇ A 9
♣ 10 6 5 3

♠ J 7 3
♡ Q J 9 4
◇ Q 3
♣ 9 7 4 2

Teams. North–South vulnerable
Dealer East

WEST	NORTH	EAST	SOUTH
		No bid	1♡(1)
4◇	4♡(2)	All pass	

(1) At least five hearts.
(2) Not a universal choice.

1. West led the jack of clubs: three–two–**ace**.
2. **Ace** of hearts led: three–six–four.
3. **King** of hearts led: eight–ten–nine.
4. Two of hearts from declarer: ◇8 *from West*–♠2 *from dummy* . . .

PLAN EAST'S DEFENCE.

5. Suppose after winning the heart, East led ◇Q: 4–10–9.

HOW SHOULD EAST NOW PROCEED?

HOW THE PLAY WENT:

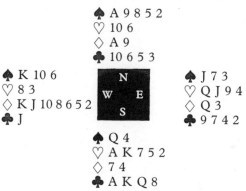

♠ A 9 8 5 2
♡ 10 6
◇ A 9
♣ 10 6 5 3

♠ K 10 6
♡ 8 3
◇ K J 10 8 6 5 2
♣ J

♠ J 7 3
♡ Q J 9 4
◇ Q 3
♣ 9 7 4 2

♠ Q 4
♡ A K 7 5 2
◇ 7 4
♣ A K Q 8

South read the lead as a probable singleton and immediately played three rounds of trumps. East won the third and led the queen of diamonds, ducked all round. The ◇A won the second diamond and declarer cashed out the clubs, ending in hand, and then led another heart. East won and led his low spade–queen–king and declarer could not avoid a spade loser for one down.

WHAT ERRORS, IF ANY, WERE COMMITTED?

Solution:

On the defence found by East, declarer had a chance to make the contract and guessed correctly to land his game. This was in fact the hand:

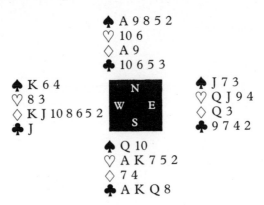

♠ A 9 8 5 2
♡ 10 6
◇ A 9
♣ 10 6 5 3

♠ K 6 4   ♠ J 7 3
♡ 8 3   ♡ Q J 9 4
◇ K J 10 8 6 5 2   ◇ Q 3
♣ J   ♣ 9 7 4 2

♠ Q 10
♡ A K 7 5 2
◇ 7 4
♣ A K Q 8

After ♣A, ♡A, ♡K and a third heart, East played the ◇Q and was left on lead. At that stage East should have cashed his other heart before playing a second diamond. When he failed to do that but played a second diamond at once, declarer ran his clubs and put East on lead with a heart. East led a low spade and South guessed correctly, inserting the ten and forcing West's king. Had East rid himself of the thrown-in card no such endplay could have arisen.

On the above hand declarer could, in fact, have succeeded regardless of the defence. The winning line is to win the queen of diamonds return with the ace, run the clubs, and then exit with the second diamond. If East is able to win the second diamond, he can cash another heart but is then end-played in spades, while if West wins the second diamond and continues the suit, South ruffs and leads a trump, again end-playing East. Declarer will take the right view in spades, reasoning that competent defenders would not allow themselves to be end-played unless they had no alternative. (In other words, if East held the ♠K West would not leave East on play but would win the second diamond and lead a spade, not a third diamond.)

If East cashed his second trump winner before leading the queen of diamonds, South would win, run the clubs and then cash his last trump, reducing West to a singleton diamond before throwing him in to lead away from the king of spades.

37. QUICK ON THE DRAW

♠ A Q J
♡ J 5
◇ A Q 10 5 4
♣ Q 7 5

Rubber bridge. East–West vulnerable
Dealer West

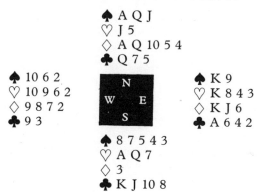

WEST	NORTH	EAST	SOUTH
No bid	1NT(1)	No bid	2♠(2)
No bid	3♠	No bid	4♠
No bid	No bid	No bid	

♠ 8 7 5 4 3
♡ A Q 7
◇ 3
♣ K J 10 8

(1) 15–17.
(2) Natural and forcing.

1. West led the nine of clubs: five–**ace**–eight.
2. East returned the two of clubs: jack–three . . .

HOW SHOULD SOUTH PLAN THE PLAY?

HOW THE PLAY WENT:

♠ A Q J
♡ J 5
◇ A Q 10 5 4
♣ Q 7 5

♠ 10 6 2
♡ 10 9 6 2
◇ 9 8 7 2
♣ 9 3

♠ K 9
♡ K 8 4 3
◇ K J 6
♣ A 6 4 2

♠ 8 7 5 4 3
♡ A Q 7
◇ 3
♣ K J 10 8

The nine of clubs went to the ace and the ♣2 was returned. South won with the jack and took the spade finesse. East won the king of spades and returned the four of clubs for West to ruff. West then switched to a diamond but declarer won with the ace, took the heart finesse (jack–king–ace), cashed the ace of hearts and ruffed a heart in dummy. The ace of spades drew the remaining trumps and declarer claimed.

WHAT MISTAKES, IF ANY, WERE MADE AND BY WHOM?

Solution:
Declarer in practice failed by following the line of play given for this was the actual deal:

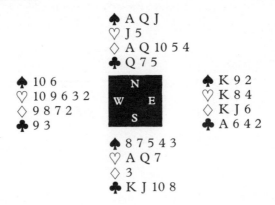

♠ A Q J
♡ J 5
◇ A Q 10 5 4
♣ Q 7 5

♠ 10 6
♡ 10 9 6 3 2
◇ 9 8 7 2
♣ 9 3

♠ K 9 2
♡ K 8 4
◇ K J 6
♣ A 6 4 2

♠ 8 7 5 4 3
♡ A Q 7
◇ 3
♣ K J 10 8

As the play went (♣A, club back, spade finesse, club ruff, diamond switch), declarer could and should have made comfortably. When he in fact took the heart ruff in dummy, East's ♠9 became promoted to be the setting trick. However, after winning the ◇A, South should continue by ruffing a second diamond, crossing to the ♠Q (when West shows out the heart ruff play is known to be a disaster) and ruffing a third diamond. On the actual cards, the ◇K has now fallen and declarer draws the last trump and claims.

If the second round of trumps had drawn the remaining trumps, so that the heart ruff plan is now viable, declarer would have to choose while in dummy whether to take the heart finesse or whether to try to drop the king of diamonds on the third round. He cannot combine his chances since the only way back to dummy now is with the third spade. The appearance of the ◇J may persuade declarer to go for dropping the ◇K, not usually the better chance.

Declarer's main error, however, came much earlier. After winning the jack of clubs, South should refuse to take the spade finesse. The correct line, catering for most possibilities, is to lead a spade to the ace at trick three and continue with the queen of spades. On the actual layout above, East wins the ♠K but cannot give West a club ruff. Declarer now makes easily. Further, if West began with K–x or K–x–x in spades, refusing the spade finesse does not jeopardise the contract. West can win the ♠K but cannot give East the lead so that again declarer can draw the last trump and make with ease.

There is strong evidence that East has the ♠K (East won the ♣A and returned a club rather than ducking the club, suggesting that East is confident of getting the lead) and even if East began with ♠K–x and West with ♠x–x–x, playing ace and another spade is not inferior in any way to the spade finesse play.

38. TAKE ME TO YOUR LEADER

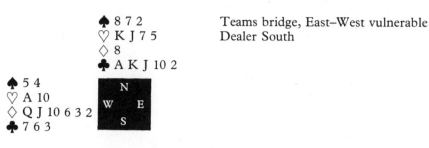

♠ 8 7 2
♡ K J 7 5
◇ 8
♣ A K J 10 2

Teams bridge, East–West vulnerable
Dealer South

♠ 5 4
♡ A 10
◇ Q J 10 6 3 2
♣ 7 6 3

SOUTH	WEST	NORTH	EAST
1◇	No bid	2♣	No bid
2NT*	No bid	3NT	All pass

* Shows minimum opening, denies three clubs. North-South
play '5-card majors, better minor'.

WHAT SHOULD WEST LEAD?

HOW THE PLAY WENT:

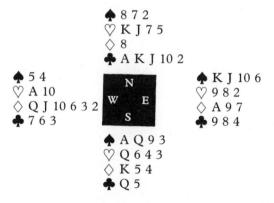

♠ 8 7 2
♡ K J 7 5
◇ 8
♣ A K J 10 2

♠ 5 4
♡ A 10
◇ Q J 10 6 3 2
♣ 7 6 3

♠ K J 10 6
♡ 9 8 2
◇ A 9 7
♣ 9 8 4

♠ A Q 9 3
♡ Q 6 4 3
◇ K 5 4
♣ Q 5

West led the queen of diamonds to his partner's ace. East returned the
nine of diamonds, low from declarer and low from West. The third
diamond was won by declarer's king. Declarer led a low heart but West
rose with the ace and cashed the remaining diamonds for down two.

WHAT ERRORS WERE MADE?

YES, BUT WHAT ERRORS WERE MADE APART FROM THE BIDDING?

Solution:

North–South should clearly reach four hearts and not 3NT. If South is required to bid 2NT, then North should take the opportunity to rebid 3♡.

In real life 3NT was reached, and the contract succeeded as the complete layout was as follows:

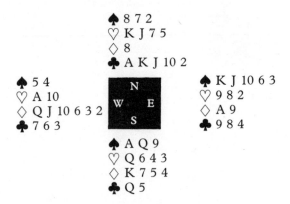

♠ 8 7 2
♡ K J 7 5
◇ 8
♣ A K J 10 2

♠ 5 4
♡ A 10
◇ Q J 10 6 3 2
♣ 7 6 3

♠ K J 10 6 3
♡ 9 8 2
◇ A 9
♣ 9 8 4

♠ A Q 9
♡ Q 6 4 3
◇ K 7 5 4
♣ Q 5

West's ◇Q lead was taken by the ace and the nine of diamonds was returned, South playing low. West was obliged to play low, for had he overtaken and returned a diamond South would have made an extra trick with the seven.

Left on lead, East switched to the jack of spades. South rose with the ace (although the spade finesse would have worked it was dangerous, for West might have gained the lead to knock out the king of diamonds) and led a heart. West took the ace of hearts and returned a spade but declarer had nine tricks.

The basic error was West's opening lead. Although it is normal to lead the top of a sequence, when the suit has been bid by an opponent and the sequence is only three cards long one should prefer to lead the fourth-highest (or at least a low card). On the lead of a low diamond declarer has no chance, for West is able to overtake the return of the nine of diamonds and continue the suit, with the ace of hearts as a re-entry. More might then have been said about the North–South bidding.

EXPERT LEVEL
DEALS 39 TO 57

39. LET HIM WHO IS WITHOUT SIN ...

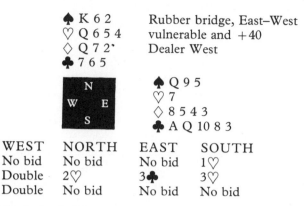

♠ K 6 2   Rubber bridge, East–West
♡ Q 6 5 4   vulnerable and +40
♢ Q 7 2˙   Dealer West
♣ 7 6 5

♠ Q 9 5
♡ 7
♢ 8 5 4 3
♣ A Q 10 8 3

WEST	NORTH	EAST	SOUTH
No bid	No bid	No bid	1♡
Double	2♡	3♣	3♡
Double	No bid	No bid	No bid

1. West led the jack of clubs ...

HOW SHOULD EAST TACKLE THE DEFENCE?

HOW THE PLAY WENT:

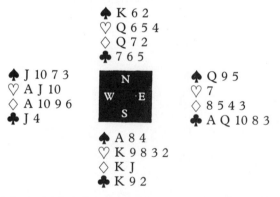

♠ K 6 2
♡ Q 6 5 4
♢ Q 7 2
♣ 7 6 5

♠ J 10 7 3
♡ A J 10
♢ A 10 9 6
♣ J 4

♠ Q 9 5
♡ 7
♢ 8 5 4 3
♣ A Q 10 8 3

♠ A 8 4
♡ K 9 8 3 2
♢ K J
♣ K 9 2

West led the jack of clubs won by East's ace. The ♣Q return was taken by South with the king. South led a heart to the queen which won and a heart back, ducked to West's jack. West cashed the ace of hearts and led a spade. South won the ♠A and led the ♢K, taken by the ace. The next spade was won by dummy's king, a low diamond went to South's jack and declarer, having kept the ♡2, was able to cross to dummy's six and use the ♢Q for a discard of a black loser. South, in fact, threw a spade but could not avoid losing a club later. One down, losing two hearts, a diamond and two clubs.

WHAT MISTAKES, IF ANY, WERE MADE?

Solution:
West's take-out double with only a doubleton holding in clubs and a three-card holding in the enemy suit was no thing of joy and the penalty double of 3♡ was even worse, despite the result. West could not be sure of defeating 3♡, and at rubber, speculative doubles into game are reserved for those with friendly bank managers and unlimited overdrafts.

As an honour card is led normally only from a sequence or from shortage, East knew from his own ten of clubs, that West's lead of the jack of clubs was the latter. While it is often difficult to tell whether partner has led a singleton or a doubleton, West's takeout double, strange as it was, would have been ludicrous with a singleton in clubs and East should have played for the more likely holding of jack doubleton. If East ducks the first round of clubs, West can continue clubs when in with the ace of diamonds and 3♡ is defeated for certain.

On the actual play, after winning the ♣K at trick two South should have made 3♡ doubled. The high card position was pretty well marked from the original passes and subsequent actions and West's double of 3♡ indicated quite clearly that hearts were not breaking 2–2. After the ♡Q won in dummy, the second round of hearts was futile.

Instead, declarer should then have tackled diamonds leading low to his king. West can win and lead a spade but South wins the ace, cashes the jack of diamonds and crosses to the king of spades in this ending:

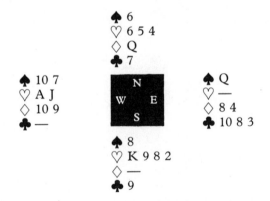

South discards his spade on the ◇Q, then ruffs dummy's spade and leads a heart. West can take the two heart tricks but then must concede a ruff-and-discard allowing South to rid himself of the club loser. That would be a salutary lesson to West about doubles into game at rubber bridge.

On this deal, only dummy would be able to cast stones.

40. CAUSE TO PAUSE

Rubber bridge, neither side vulnerable
Dealer South

SOUTH	WEST	NORTH	EAST
1♠	No bid	4NT	No bid
5◇	No bid	5♠	No bid
No bid*	No bid		

*After a considerable pause

What should West lead from

♠ 6 3
♡ A 8
◇ J 8 7 5 2
♣ A 9 3 2

In practice, West led the ace of hearts and this was the dummy:

♠ K Q 9 2
♡ 7
◇ A K 10 9 3
♣ K 8 5

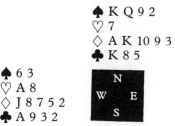

♠ 6 3
♡ A 8
◇ J 8 7 5 2
♣ A 9 3 2

1. West led the **ace of hearts**: seven–two–five.

HOW SHOULD WEST CONTINUE?

HOW THE PLAY WENT:

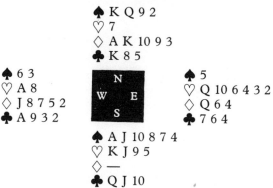

♠ K Q 9 2
♡ 7
◇ A K 10 9 3
♣ K 8 5

♠ 6 3
♡ A 8
◇ J 8 7 5 2
♣ A 9 3 2

♠ 5
♡ Q 10 6 4 3 2
◇ Q 6 4
♣ 7 6 4

♠ A J 10 8 7 4
♡ K J 9 5
◇ —
♣ Q J 10

At trick two West switched to a trump. Declarer won ♠K, came to ♠A and led the jack of clubs. West played low and the jack won the trick. A heart was ruffed in dummy and South discarded his remaining clubs on the diamonds. Making six when the other heart loser was ruffed.

HOW MANY MISTAKES WERE MADE ON THIS DEAL?

Solution:
With the spade switch at trick two West virtually gave up on defeating the contract. While one cannot guarantee defeat, the best chance at trick two is a low club. This was the complete deal:

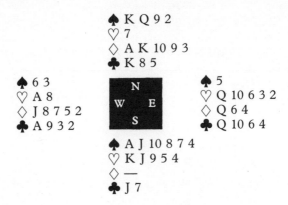

                    ♠ K Q 9 2
                    ♡ 7
                    ◇ A K 10 9 3
                    ♣ K 8 5

♠ 6 3   ♠ 5
♡ A 8   ♡ Q 10 6 3 2
◇ J 8 7 5 2   ◇ Q 6 4
♣ A 9 3 2   ♣ Q 10 6 4

                    ♠ A J 10 8 7 4
                    ♡ K J 9 5 4
                    ◇ —
                    ♣ J 7

On any defence but a low club at trick two declarer has a very easy time as he can discard his club losers on the A–K of diamonds and crossruff the rest of the hand.

The clue to this defence lies in South's long trance after North had used Blackwood and signed off in 5♠, a clear sign that two aces were missing. The only factor that could give South cause to pause would be a void. A void in clubs would be of no use to the defence but if South were void in diamonds, it would be vital to take two club tricks before declarer can use the diamond discards.

The low club requires South to pick the club position in order to make the hand. That is the best the defence can do.

41. THE SLENDER THREAD

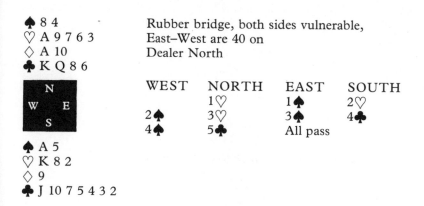

♠ 8 4
♡ A 9 7 6 3
◇ A 10
♣ K Q 8 6

Rubber bridge, both sides vulnerable,
East–West are 40 on
Dealer North

WEST	NORTH	EAST	SOUTH
	1♡	1♠	2♡
2♠	3♡	3♠	4♣
4♠	5♣	All pass	

♠ A 5
♡ K 8 2
◇ 9
♣ J 10 7 5 4 3 2

1. West led the two of spades: four–queen–**ace**

HOW SHOULD SOUTH PLAN THE PLAY?

HOW THE PLAY WENT:

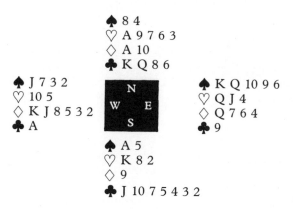

♠ 8 4
♡ A 9 7 6 3
◇ A 10
♣ K Q 8 6

♠ J 7 3 2
♡ 10 5
◇ K J 8 5 3 2
♣ A

♠ K Q 10 9 6
♡ Q J 4
◇ Q 7 6 4
♣ 9

♠ A 5
♡ K 8 2
◇ 9
♣ J 10 7 5 4 3 2

South won the ace of spades and returned a spade, won by East who switched to a low diamond: nine–jack–**ace**. Declarer ruffed a diamond and led a club, won by West who did not fall into the trap of conceding a ruff and discard. West led a heart and declarer could not avoid a heart loser. One down.

WHAT ERRORS WERE COMMITTED?

Solution:
Declarer in fact made his contract when the defence slipped up. The play
went as described up to trick four: ♣2 won by South's ace, spade back to
East, diamond switch won by the ace and a diamond ruffed.

At trick five, declarer did not make the mistake of leading a club. He
first cashed the ace and king of hearts and only then led a club in this
position:

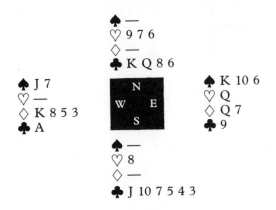

West won the ♣A and could not avoid giving declarer a ruff-and-
discard, allowing South to pitch his heart loser. West could have avoided
this by winning the jack of spades at trick two and cashing the ♣A to
avoid being endplayed with the bare ace later. This was all foreseeable for
West who had to ask himself why South was making the unusual play of a
spade at trick two. The bidding marked South with three hearts and at
least six clubs (he did not revert to 5♡ over 5♣) and even if East did not
hold the likely five spades for his overcall, there was no urgency for South
to be looking for a spade ruff so that he must be planning an elimination.
To thwart the throw-in, rid yourself of the throw-in card.

Did you spot declarer's error? It is slightly superior to duck the first
spade rather than win the ace and return a spade as the latter play is more
likely to arouse suspicion with the defenders.

42. NOT REASONABLE

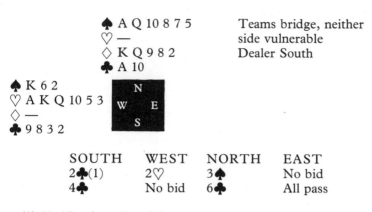

♠ A Q 10 8 7 5
♡ —
◇ K Q 9 8 2
♣ A 10

Teams bridge, neither
side vulnerable
Dealer South

♠ K 6 2
♡ A K Q 10 5 3
◇ —
♣ 9 8 3 2

SOUTH	WEST	NORTH	EAST
2♣(1)	2♡	3♠	No bid
4♣	No bid	6♣	All pass

(1) 11–15 points, 5+ clubs.

1. West led the king of hearts, ruffed by the ♣10, East dropping the four.
2. The ♣A was cashed, East following with the six.

HOW SHOULD WEST PLAN THE DEFENCE?

HOW THE PLAY WENT:

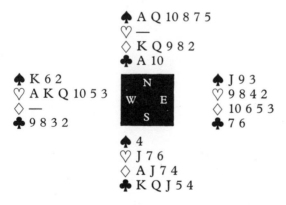

♠ A Q 10 8 7 5
♡ —
◇ K Q 9 8 2
♣ A 10

♠ K 6 2
♡ A K Q 10 5 3
◇ —
♣ 9 8 3 2

♠ J 9 3
♡ 9 8 4 2
◇ 10 6 5 3
♣ 7 6

♠ 4
♡ J 7 6
◇ A J 7 4
♣ K Q J 5 4

Declarer ruffed the heart lead, cashed the ace of clubs and the ace of spades. He then ruffed a second spade and drew trumps. Declarer discarded a heart loser on the fifth round of diamonds but as the king of spades had not fallen, declarer could not use dummy's spade suit and had to concede a loser at the end. Making just six.

WHAT ERRORS, IF ANY, WERE COMMITTED?

Solution:

The actual layout was that given and had declarer followed the given line of play, he would have succeeded comfortably in making his slam. In fact, declarer went two off on the hand, although he played reasonably. What happened that made declarer fail?

As soon as dummy ruffs the heart lead, West can envisage what is going to happen and when declarer cashes the ace of spades, East following with the three, West should already be prepared to drop the king of spades without any dithering. That is what actually happened at the table. South gave West a wary look but if the king of spades were really a singleton, it would be dangerous for South to play another spade as that could promote a trump trick for the defenders, while if he tried to cash the ♠Q, discarding a heart, and that were ruffed the opposition could then cash another heart.

Taken in by West's smooth play of the king of spades, declarer attempted to return to hand with a diamond. West pounced on that with a trump and cashed two hearts for down two.

The North–South bidding leaves a lot to be desired but their reaching of six clubs instead of the frigid seven diamonds is the concern of their teammates.

43. ANY TWO WILL DO

♠ J 9 7 5 4　　Teams bridge, East–West vulnerable
♡ 5 3　　　　 Dealer East
♢ J 7 2
♣ Q J 5

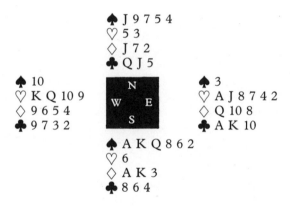

WEST	NORTH	EAST	SOUTH
		1♡	2♠
3♡	4♠	All pass	

♠ A K Q 8 6 2
♡ 6
♢ A K 3
♣ 8 6 4

1. West led the **king of hearts**: five–eight–six.
2. West continued with the queen of hearts . . ..

HOW SHOULD SOUTH PLAN THE PLAY?

HOW THE PLAY WENT:

```
               ♠ J 9 7 5 4
               ♡ 5 3
               ♢ J 7 2
               ♣ Q J 5
♠ 10                           ♠ 3
♡ K Q 10 9      N              ♡ A J 8 7 4 2
♢ 9 6 5 4     W   E            ♢ Q 10 8
♣ 9 7 3 2       S              ♣ A K 10
               ♠ A K Q 8 6 2
               ♡ 6
               ♢ A K 3
               ♣ 8 6 4
```

South ruffed the second round of hearts and drew trumps. He then cashed the ace and king of diamonds followed by a third diamond to the jack and queen. East cashed the ace and king of clubs. One down.

WHAT ERRORS, IF ANY WERE COMMITTED?

Solution:

If 4♠ were a certain make, East–West might sacrifice in 5♡ but East had sufficient defensive potential to hope that 4♠ would fail. North's jump to 4♠ was intended as much as an advance sacrifice as anything else. With 4♡ a possible make for East–West, especially as North's spade length would rob South of defensive tricks there, North bid 4♠ with the hope of making, secure in the knowledge that it would hardly prove expensive.

In fact, 4♠ succeeded on the line taken by declarer. Can you tell what the not too improbable layout was?

This was the actual hand:

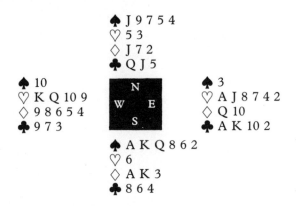

```
                  ♠ J 9 7 5 4
                  ♡ 5 3
                  ◇ J 7 2
                  ♣ Q J 5
  ♠ 10                          ♠ 3
  ♡ K Q 10 9          N         ♡ A J 8 7 4 2
  ◇ 9 8 6 5 4     W       E     ◇ Q 10
  ♣ 9 7 3             S         ♣ A K 10 2
                  ♠ A K Q 8 6 2
                  ♡ 6
                  ◇ A K 3
                  ♣ 8 6 4
```

South ruffed the second heart, drew trumps and the ◇A–K dropped East's queen. A diamond went to the jack and a trump back to hand allowed declarer to endplay East via a club to the jack.

4♠ can be beaten on an initial club lead or a top heart lead followed by a club switch. From declarer's point of view, East was marked with the A–K of clubs pretty surely once West had shown up with the K–Q of hearts. If the queen of diamonds was not doubleton, the contract was bound to fail, since declarer would have to lose a heart and two clubs as well as the diamond, unless East happened to have started with the ◇Q and A–K doubleton of clubs. Then he could be endplayed by tackling clubs first.

Declarer's decision rested between playing East for a doubleton diamond or a doubleton club.

44. THE LADY IS A TRAMP

♠ K 10 6　　　　　　　　　　　Teams bridge, both sides
♡ Q 6 4　　　　　　　　　　　vulnerable
♢ A J 6　　　　　　　　　　　Dealer North
♣ 8 7 4 3

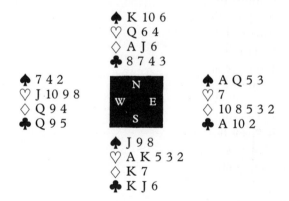

♠ A Q 5 3
♡ 7
♢ 10 8 5 3 2
♣ A 10 2

WEST	NORTH	EAST	SOUTH
	No bid	No bid	1♡(1)
No bid	2♡	Double	No bid
2♠	3♡	All pass	

(1) North–South play five-card majors.

1. West led the jack of hearts: **queen**–seven–two.
2. Four of hearts from dummy: *diamond discard*–**ace of hearts**–♡8
3. Nine of spades from South: two–six . . ..

HOW SHOULD EAST CONTINUE THE DEFENCE?

HOW THE PLAY WENT:

♠ K 10 6
♡ Q 6 4
♢ A J 6
♣ 8 7 4 3

♠ 7 4 2　　　　　　　　　　　　　♠ A Q 5 3
♡ J 10 9 8　　　　　　　　　　　♡ 7
♢ Q 9 4　　　　　　　　　　　　♢ 10 8 5 3 2
♣ Q 9 5　　　　　　　　　　　　♣ A 10 2

♠ J 9 8
♡ A K 5 3 2
♢ K 7
♣ K J 6

After winning the ♠Q at trick three, East switched to the two of clubs.
Declarer considered that for quite some time but finally inserted the
jack. West won the queen of clubs and returned a club. East took the ♣A
and the ♠A and West still had a trump trick for down one.

WHAT MISTAKES WERE MADE AND WHO MADE THEM?

Solution:
In the bidding North might have preferred no-trumps bids instead of either of his heart raises. The comfort afforded by playing five-card majors leads a number of players into blindly supporting the major even when the hand pattern indicates the desirability of no-trumps.

When the hand was actually played, declarer made 3♡ as this was the layout:

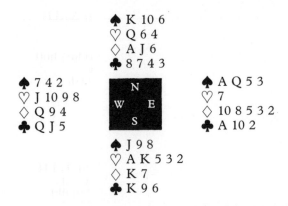

```
            ♠ K 10 6
            ♡ Q 6 4
            ◇ A J 6
            ♣ 8 7 4 3
♠ 7 4 2        N        ♠ A Q 5 3
♡ J 10 9 8              ♡ 7
◇ Q 9 4     W     E     ◇ 10 8 5 3 2
♣ Q J 5                 ♣ A 10 2
               S
            ♠ J 9 8
            ♡ A K 5 3 2
            ◇ K 7
            ♣ K 9 6
```

After two rounds of hearts, declarer led the ♠9 to East's queen but when East returned a low club, South rose with the king, figuring that if the ♣A were wrong there was little chance for the contract anyway. When the ♣K held, declarer cashed a third round of hearts and then played ◇K and a diamond to the jack. The finesse had to work if declarer was going to make 3♡ and when it did, declarer discarded a club on the ◇A and conceded a spade and a heart.

It was equally obvious to East after trick two that West held a trump trick and the possibility that West might have responded to the double in a three-card suit was confirmed when West followed to the ♠9 with the deuce. That also marked the ♠J with South for West would have covered the nine with the jack if possible. Thus East should have won the first spade trick with the ace and not with the queen.

There is no reason why South should not believe the spade finesse is working and now when the ♣2 switch comes and South rises with the ♣K, there would be no reason why South should risk the diamond finesse. When the spade finesse is repeated, declarer is one down. If South wins the ♣K and plays a second club before returning to spades West will have to win the club and lead a spade, lest declarer establish the thirteenth club for a spade discard.

Declarer may smell a rat at that stage but there is no other reasonable chance for the defence.

45. PENDULUM PLAYS

♠ A J
♡ A Q 9 8 3
◇ Q J 5
♣ K J 6

Rubber bridge, both sides vulnerable
Dealer South

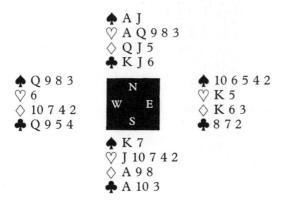

SOUTH	WEST	NORTH	EAST
1♡	No bid	3♡(1)	No bid
4♡	No bid	4NT	No bid
5♡	No bid	6♡	All pass

♠ K 7
♡ J 10 7 4 2
◇ A 9 8
♣ A 10 3

(1) Forcing.

West led the two of diamonds: queen–king–**ace**.

HOW SHOULD SOUTH PLAN THE PLAY?

HOW THE PLAY WENT:

                ♠ A J
                ♡ A Q 9 8 3
                ◇ Q J 5
                ♣ K J 6

♠ Q 9 8 3   ♠ 10 6 5 4 2
♡ 6   N   ♡ K 5
◇ 10 7 4 2   W   E   ◇ K 6 3
♣ Q 9 5 4   S   ♣ 8 7 2

                ♠ K 7
                ♡ J 10 7 4 2
                ◇ A 9 8
                ♣ A 10 3

At trick two, South led the jack of hearts and ran it to East's king. East returned a diamond, nine, ten, jack. The last trump was drawn, a diamond played to the eight, followed by the ace of clubs and a club to the jack. When that finesse worked, declarer was home. Six hearts made.

WHAT ERRORS, IF ANY, WERE COMMITTED?

Solution:
Declarer made his slam but he deserved to fail. Had the club finesse lost, he would have gone down but he can improve his chances significantly so that, most of the time, he will not need to guess the club position.

After capturing East's king of diamonds, South should continue at trick two by leading the nine of diamonds, running it if West plays low. If the ◇9 holds or if it goes nine, ten, jack, low, declarer should play ace of hearts. If the king of hearts falls, declarer can draw the other trump and guess the clubs for an overtrick.

If hearts prove to be 3–0, declarer continues hearts and assuming the opponent wins the king of hearts and unhelpfully returns a heart, declarer will have to guess the clubs for contract. However, when hearts are 2–1 and the king is still out, the most common position, declarer cashes his two spades and his diamond winner and then plays a heart, putting the ♡K on lead. That opponent will then have to open up the clubs or concede a ruff-and-discard.

On the given hand, that play would work regardless of the location of the queen of clubs. Thus declarer's heart finesse at trick two was a definite error.

Note that to run the ◇9 at trick two is almost without risk. West's ◇2 lead suggests his holding the ten and if it happens to be a singleton two, South had a diamond loser anyway and if West ruffs the ◇9, nothing significant has been lost. If the ◇9 did lose to the ◇10, then the odds favour finessing in hearts and later clubs will have to be guessed.

However, there was a serious error by the defence. East could also tell that West had led from 10–x–x–x and he should not have covered the ◇Q at trick one. That play could not gain and might lose. If East plays a low diamond at trick one, South's slam must fail unless declarer plays the hand double dummy (eliminate spades, finesse against West for the ♣Q, eliminate clubs and then play ace and another heart). More commonly, declarer would take the heart finesse and then East could exit with anything but a diamond and declarer will fail.

46. WHAT'S GOING ON HERE?

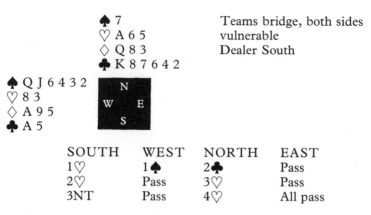

♠ 7
♡ A 6 5
◇ Q 8 3
♣ K 8 7 6 4 2

Teams bridge, both sides
vulnerable
Dealer South

♠ Q J 6 4 3 2
♡ 8 3
◇ A 9 5
♣ A 5

SOUTH	WEST	NORTH	EAST
1♡	1♠	2♣	Pass
2♡	Pass	3♡	Pass
3NT	Pass	4♡	All pass

1. West led the four of spades: seven–nine–**ten**.
2. South led the ♣3: West won the **ace**–two–nine.

HOW SHOULD WEST CONTINUE?

HOW THE PLAY WENT:

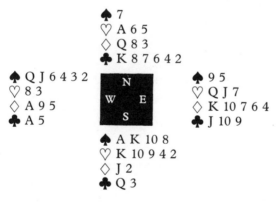

♠ 7
♡ A 6 5
◇ Q 8 3
♣ K 8 7 6 4 2

♠ Q J 6 4 3 2
♡ 8 3
◇ A 9 5
♣ A 5

♠ 9 5
♡ Q J 7
◇ K 10 7 6 4
♣ J 10 9

♠ A K 10 8
♡ K 10 9 4 2
◇ J 2
♣ Q 3

Not wishing to open a new suit or possibly trap a trump honour with East, West exited with his remaining club, ducked to South's queen. South then cashed the king of hearts and led a heart to the ace. On the king of clubs South discarded one diamond and on the next club, South's second diamond went away as East trumped in.

Declarer thus lost just one trump and one club, his remaining spade loser being trumped in dummy.

WHAT ERRORS WERE MADE DURING THE PLAY?

Solution:

DEFENSIVE ERRORS:
1. West might have preferred a trump lead, indicated by North's reluctance to play no-trumps.
2. After winning the ace of clubs (not unreasonable), West had a marked switch to the ace of diamonds. The play to the first trick marked South with ♠ A–K–10–8 (East's nine denied the eight). South was also marked with five hearts from the bidding, leaving him with at most four minor cards. If South held the ◇K, the defence could not come to more than one diamond trick so that West had nothing to lose and everything to gain by switching to the ◇A at trick three (notwithstanding East's error).
3. East erred by dropping the nine of clubs at trick two instead of the jack (denying the queen). That does not excuse West's error since if South did hold a singleton club, East's ♣9 was known to be the wrong card.

DESPITE ALL THE ABOVE ASSISTANCE FROM THE DEFENCE, DECLARER FAILED BY ONE TRICK BY FOLLOWING THE GIVEN LINE. WHAT DID DECLARER DO WRONG?

This was the actual layout:

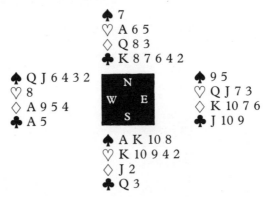

```
              ♠ 7
              ♡ A 6 5
              ◇ Q 8 3
              ♣ K 8 7 6 4 2
♠ Q J 6 4 3 2                ♠ 9 5
♡ 8              N           ♡ Q J 7 3
◇ A 9 5 4     W   E         ◇ K 10 7 6
♣ A 5             S          ♣ J 10 9
              ♠ A K 10 8
              ♡ K 10 9 4 2
              ◇ J 2
              ♣ Q 3
```

The play went as described to trick five: ♠4 won by the ten; ♣3 won by the ace; ♣5 to South's queen; king of hearts and a heart to the ace.

However, West showed out on the second round of hearts. On ♣K and the next club South discarded his two diamond losers, but East ruffed the fourth club, cashed his other top trump and left South with a spade loser.

Declarer could have guarded against the 4–1 trump break by a simple precaution: at tricks four and five, he should have led a heart to the ace and a heart back to the king, followed by the ♠8 ruffed in dummy and then the ♣K and another club. There was little risk in ruffing the second spade. With seven spades West might have bid more than 1♠ and West led the four of spades, marking him with six spades at most and East therefore with two spades at least.

106

47. A BABY GRAND

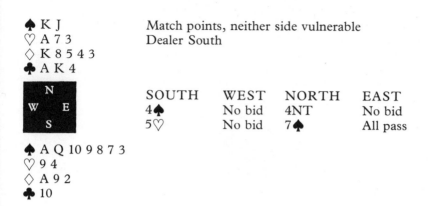

♠ K J
♡ A 7 3
◇ K 8 5 4 3
♣ A K 4

Match points, neither side vulnerable
Dealer South

SOUTH	WEST	NORTH	EAST
4♠	No bid	4NT	No bid
5♡	No bid	7♠	All pass

♠ A Q 10 9 8 7 3
♡ 9 4
◇ A 9 2
♣ 10

1. West led the eight of clubs: **ace**–seven–ten.

HOW SHOULD SOUTH PLAN THE PLAY?

HOW THE PLAY WENT:

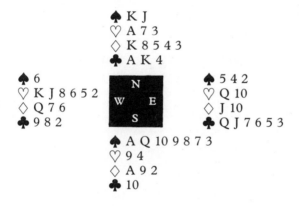

♠ K J
♡ A 7 3
◇ K 8 5 4 3
♣ A K 4

♠ 6
♡ K J 8 6 5 2
◇ Q 7 6
♣ 9 8 2

♠ 5 4 2
♡ Q 10
◇ J 10
♣ Q J 7 6 5 3

♠ A Q 10 9 8 7 3
♡ 9 4
◇ A 9 2
♣ 10

After the ace of clubs won, declarer drew trumps in three rounds, discarding a heart from dummy and West discarding the 6–2 of hearts. Then came the ace of diamonds followed by a diamond to the king. On the king of clubs South pitched his diamond loser and set up the diamonds by ruffing the third round. Over to the ace of hearts for a heart discard on the diamonds saw the grand slam home.

WHAT MISTAKES IF ANY TOOK PLACE?

Solution:
West's lead of a club rather than the normal trump lead against a grand slam did not cost and on this bidding it may be dangerous to lead a trump. Declarer in fact failed in his grand slam when the diamond suit did not divide conveniently 3–2. This was the layout:

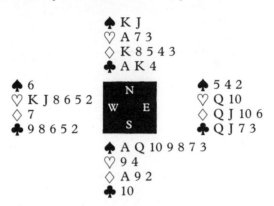

♠ K J
♡ A 7 3
◇ K 8 5 4 3
♣ A K 4

♠ 6
♡ K J 8 6 5 2
◇ 7
♣ 9 8 6 5 2

♠ 5 4 2
♡ Q 10
◇ Q J 10 6
♣ Q J 7 3

♠ A Q 10 9 8 7 3
♡ 9 4
◇ A 9 2
♣ 10

After winning the ♣8 with the ace and drawing three rounds of trumps, South cashed the ace–king of diamonds, discarded a diamond on the ♣K and ruffed a diamond. He could cross to the ace of hearts and ruff another diamond but there was no longer an entry to return to the established diamond winner.

If the diamonds are 3–2, they can be tackled early as well and it is safer to tackle them early while there is the extra entry position in dummy with the top trumps in case they do break badly (a 4–1 break occurs a little more than one time in four). The correct line after ♣A is to take one top trump from dummy and then play the ◇A and a diamond to the king. If the diamonds are 3–2, cash dummy's other top trump, discard a diamond on the ♣K and ruff a diamond. Draw any trump outstanding and claim.

If diamonds are 4–1 and the opposition have not ruffed in, take the diamond discard on the ♣A and ruff a diamond. Then cross to dummy's remaining top trump and ruff another diamond. Draw any remaining trumps and then cross to the ♡A for the diamond to discard your heart loser.

Note the slight extra safety afforded by taking just one round of trumps before starting on the diamonds. On the actual hand if the diamonds are started before any trumps are drawn, West ruffs the second round of diamonds, giving him a very good reason for not having led his trump against the grand slam.

48. FOLLOW THROUGH

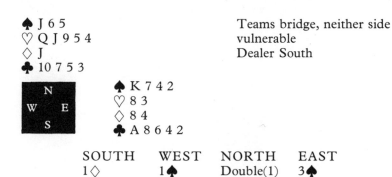

♠ J 6 5
♡ Q J 9 5 4
◇ J
♣ 10 7 5 3

Teams bridge, neither side
vulnerable
Dealer South

♠ K 7 4 2
♡ 8 3
◇ 8 4
♣ A 8 6 4 2

SOUTH	WEST	NORTH	EAST
1◇	1♠	Double(1)	3♠
5◇(2)	No bid	No bid	No bid

(1) Negative double for takeout into hearts or clubs, 6–11 points.
(2) The North–South system card reveals: "2♠/2♡/2◇ = weak twos; 2♣ = game-force or 23+ balanced."

1. West led the **ace of spades**: five–two–eight.
2. West switched to the nine of clubs: three–**ace**–queen.

HOW SHOULD EAST CONTINUE?

HOW THE PLAY WENT:

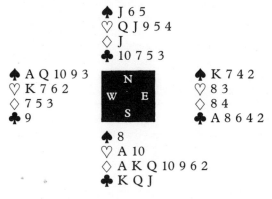

♠ J 6 5
♡ Q J 9 5 4
◇ J
♣ 10 7 5 3

♠ A Q 10 9 3
♡ K 7 6 2
◇ 7 5 3
♣ 9

♠ K 7 4 2
♡ 8 3
◇ 8 4
♣ A 8 6 4 2

♠ 8
♡ A 10
◇ A K Q 10 9 6 2
♣ K Q J

At trick three East returned the eight of clubs and West ruffed. West continued with the three of spades, six, king, ruff, and South crossed to the jack of diamonds, but when the heart finesse lost declarer was two down.

WHAT ERRORS WERE THERE?

Solution:

The defence found by East allowed declarer home when a little more thought would have found the right route. This was the actual hand:

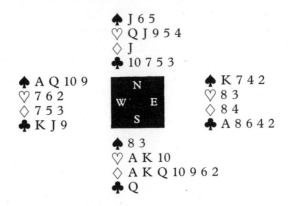

```
                    ♠ J 6 5
                    ♡ Q J 9 5 4
                    ◇ J
                    ♣ 10 7 5 3
    ♠ A Q 10 9                      ♠ K 7 4 2
    ♡ 7 6 2          N              ♡ 8 3
    ◇ 7 5 3     W         E         ◇ 8 4
    ♣ K J 9          S              ♣ A 8 6 4 2
                    ♠ 8 3
                    ♡ A K 10
                    ◇ A K Q 10 9 6 2
                    ♣ Q
```

The ♠A was led and the nine of clubs went to the ace. When East returned a club, South gratefully ruffed, drew trumps and discarded the spade loser on the fourth round of hearts. Making five diamonds.

While West's 1♠ overcall is usually expected to be of five-card length, it is not uncommon to overcall on a strong four-card holding at the one-level. Note that West can do no more than he did without grave risk. A second spade would be dangerous as East may well have five spades and if West were to switch to the king of clubs rather than the nine, the defence would almost certainly get it wrong.

The fault lay with East who assumed too quickly that West had switched to a singleton. Whenever you suspect that partner has led a singleton you should stop and consider the corollaries that follow from such an assumption. Often the consequences will be so absurd that it will be a simple matter to conclude that partner's lead could not be a singleton.

Suppose East made the assumption that South had a singleton spade and West's ♣9 was a singleton, giving South K–Q–J in clubs. What else could East deduce? There is a strong presumption that South began with seven diamonds for his leap to 5◇ without any guarantee of support opposite. If South were to have no diamond and no heart loser, South would then have to hold: ♠x ♡AK ◇AKQxxxx ♣KQJ but with such a holding South would have opened 2♣, not 1◇. Similarly if South held only six diamonds to the A–K–Q and A–K–x in hearts as well as his K–Q–J of clubs, he would be far too strong for a mere 1◇ opening. The corollary then of West having a singleton club is that South must hold a red loser and it is unnecessary to give partner a club ruff.

But what if South's club is the singleton? Then the real danger of the hand as shown above becomes apparent and it cannot cost East to lead the king of spades at trick three. If the king of spades does not survive, partner will win a trick somewhere in the red suits.

49. OUT TO AN OFF BREAK

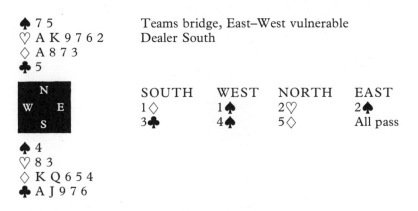

♠ 7 5 — Teams bridge, East–West vulnerable
♡ A K 9 7 6 2 — Dealer South
◇ A 8 7 3
♣ 5

SOUTH	WEST	NORTH	EAST
1◇	1♠	2♡	2♠
3♣	4♠	5◇	All pass

♠ 4
♡ 8 3
◇ K Q 6 5 4
♣ A J 9 7 6

1. West led the **king** of spades: five–ten–four.
2. West led the ace of spades: seven–three–**trumped with** ◇**4**.

HOW SHOULD SOUTH CONTINUE?

HOW THE PLAY WENT:

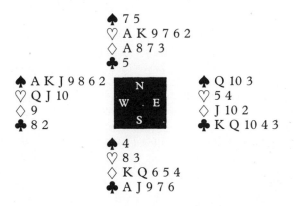

♠ 7 5
♡ A K 9 7 6 2
◇ A 8 7 3
♣ 5

♠ A K J 9 8 6 2   ♠ Q 10 3
♡ Q J 10   ♡ 5 4
◇ 9   ◇ J 10 2
♣ 8 2   ♣ K Q 10 4 3

♠ 4
♡ 8 3
◇ K Q 6 5 4
♣ A J 9 7 6

Declarer drew trumps in three rounds, followed by the ace, king and a third round of hearts ruffed. Ace of clubs and a club ruff to dummy which was now high allowed declarer to claim twelve tricks.

WHAT WERE THE ERRORS?

Solution:
Declarer in practice went one down when the hearts did not divide kindly. This was the actual hand:

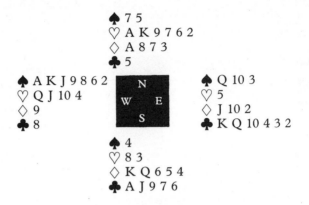

♠ 7 5
♡ A K 9 7 6 2
◇ A 8 7 3
♣ 5

♠ A K J 9 8 6 2   ♠ Q 10 3
♡ Q J 10 4   ♡ 5
◇ 9   ◇ J 10 2
♣ 8   ♣ K Q 10 4 3 2

♠ 4
♡ 8 3
◇ K Q 6 5 4
♣ A J 9 7 6

South's bidding was very aggressive but was prompted by the vulnerability. The final contract was sound. In fact, if either trumps are 2–2 or hearts 3–2, 6◇ is an excellent spot. The danger to the hand arises when trumps are 3–1 and hearts 4–1, not altogether surprising with the vulnerable opponents bidding game on less than half the points.

South ruffed the second spade and drew three rounds of trumps. Three rounds of hearts were played, declarer ruffing the third but South was now dead. He could ruff a club in dummy and set up the hearts but he could not return to them. He later lost three clubs for down two.

South would not have done better by playing just two rounds of trumps before playing off the A–K of hearts for then East ruffs the king of hearts and returns a club and South again lacks the entries to set up the hearts and return to dummy to cash them.

Correct play is to draw just one round of trumps with the king and then play ace–king of hearts. If there have been no ruffs, draw two more rounds of trumps ending in dummy and ruff a heart, claiming. If the second heart is ruffed, win the club return, cross to the ◇A drawing the only trump left and now the entries are right to set up and enjoy the hearts. If East ruffs the second heart and returns a spade, ruff *in dummy*, ruff a heart and return to dummy with a trump to the ace, ruff a heart and ruff a club to dummy, claiming. This line gains an overtrick most of the time (with hearts 3–2) without jeopardising the contract.

50. COUNTER SERVICE

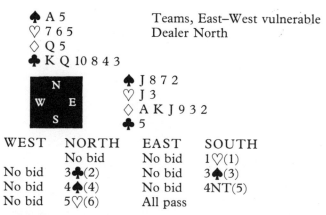

♠ A 5
♡ 7 6 5
◇ Q 5
♣ K Q 10 8 4 3

Teams, East–West vulnerable
Dealer North

♠ J 8 7 2
♡ J 3
◇ A K J 9 3 2
♣ 5

WEST	NORTH	EAST	SOUTH
	No bid	No bid	1♡(1)
No bid	3♣(2)	No bid	3♠(3)
No bid	4♠(4)	No bid	4NT(5)
No bid	5♡(6)	All pass	

(1) Five-card suit.
(2) Maximum pass, 5+ clubs and 3+ hearts.
(3) Culbertson asking bid in spades.
(4) ♠A but no other ace.
(5) Ask about heart holding.
(6) No king or queen in trumps.

1. West led the king of spades: **ace**–eight–ten.
2. Five of hearts led: three–**ace**–four.
3. **King** of hearts from South: ten–six–jack.
4. Two of hearts: West wins ♡Q, *East discards* ◇9.
5. Four of diamonds from West: five–**jack**–eight.

HOW SHOULD EAST CONTINUE?

HOW THE PLAY WENT:

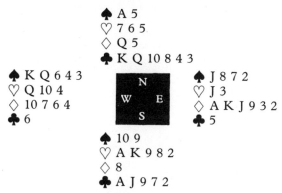

♠ A 5
♡ 7 6 5
◇ Q 5
♣ K Q 10 8 4 3

♠ K Q 6 4 3
♡ Q 10 4
◇ 10 7 6 4
♣ 6

♠ J 8 7 2
♡ J 3
◇ A K J 9 3 2
♣ 5

♠ 10 9
♡ A K 9 8 2
◇ 8
♣ A J 9 7 2

After winning the jack of diamonds, East switched back to spades thus defeating the contract by one trick.

WERE THERE ANY MISTAKES MADE?

Solution:
South's bidding was adventurous opposite a passed partner. He was looking for a slam in clubs if North could provide something like: ♠Axx ♡QJx ◇xx ♣Kxxxx, but when North denied the ♡Q, South had to give up in 5♡. An immediate 4♡ over 3♣ would have been safer. South could do no better in the play than give East–West the problem of how to cash out.

Although East solved the problem on the hand given, the defence set itself a number of obstacles. East reasoned that with one spade and two diamonds, South's first ask might have been in diamonds, not spades (a reasonable assumption but it is not generally wise to rely on the opponents) and that with six spades to the K–Q, West might have overcalled over 1♡.

However, West may have declined to overcall opposite a passed partner with no more than ♠ K Q 9 6 4 3 ♡ Q 10 4 ◇ 10 7 4 ♣6, especially at unfavourable vulnerability. If West did have that hand and the defence went the same way, declarer would have made his contract.

Error 1: On the third round of hearts, East should have confirmed his count in spades by discarding the two of spades. Although it is not standard to give the count at trick one except for specific situations, when it is obvious that the problem is to cash up the defence tricks, first priority is given to count. The eight of spades might have done no more than indicate the presence of the ♠J, but the later *two* of spades would indicate *present count* (lowest = odd number of cards left).

Error 2: If West judged that East held an even number of spades, he should have cashed the queen of spades before switching to diamonds. (If partner is given a chance to go wrong, partner will often take that chance.)

Error 3: After winning the jack of diamonds, East should have cashed a second diamond on the basis that *West's failure to cash the queen of spades indicated that the spade was not cashing*. West in fact held the 6–3–3–1 hand.

51. EASY DOES IT

♠ J
♡ A 5 4
◇ K J 6
♣ A Q 10 7 6 5

Rubber bridge, both sides vulnerable
Dealer North

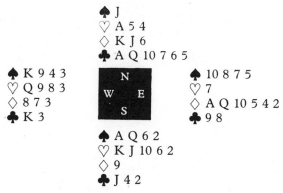

WEST	NORTH	EAST	SOUTH
	1♣	1◇	1♡
No bid	2♡	No bid	4♡
No bid	No bid	No bid	

♠ A Q 6 2
♡ K J 10 6 2
◇ 9
♣ J 4 2

1. West led the seven of diamonds: six–**ten**–nine.
2. East returned the five of spades: **ace**–four–jack.
3. Four of clubs: three–**queen**–nine.
4. **Ace of hearts**: seven–two–three.
5. Four of hearts: *East discards* ◇2–**jack of hearts**–eight.

HOW SHOULD SOUTH CONTINUE?

HOW THE PLAY WENT:

                    ♠ J
                    ♡ A 5 4
                    ◇ K J 6
                    ♣ A Q 10 7 6 5
♠ K 9 4 3   ♠ 10 8 7 5
♡ Q 9 8 3   N   ♡ 7
◇ 8 7 3   W   E   ◇ A Q 10 5 4 2
♣ K 3   S   ♣ 9 8
                    ♠ A Q 6 2
                    ♡ K J 10 6 2
                    ◇ 9
                    ♣ J 4 2

After West allowed declarer's jack of hearts to hold, South continued with the jack of clubs, king, ace, followed by a diamond ruff and a spade ruff and a third diamond ruff. The king of hearts was then cashed, leaving West with K–9 of spades and a trump. When declarer led his club, West trumped but had to give declarer his tenth trick via the queen of spades. Declarer lost just one spade, one heart and one diamond.

WHAT MISTAKES, IF ANY, WERE MADE?

Solution:
The line adopted by declarer looks quite pretty. Unfortunately it also led
to disaster when the actual hand looked like this:

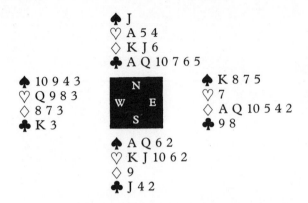

♠ J
♡ A 5 4
◇ K J 6
♣ A Q 10 7 6 5

♠ 10 9 4 3
♡ Q 9 8 3
◇ 8 7 3
♣ K 3

♠ K 8 7 5
♡ 7
◇ A Q 10 5 4 2
♣ 9 8

♠ A Q 6 2
♡ K J 10 6 2
◇ 9
♣ J 4 2

In the three card ending, East kept the king and another spade and a
diamond. When at trick eleven South led his club and West ruffed, East
discarded the spade and won the last two tricks with the ♠K and a
diamond. One down.

Declarer could have succeeded with a much simpler plan without the
necessity of picking East to have the king of spades. At trick six South
leads the jack of clubs, king, ace. Once the clubs are set up and ready to
run, South plays a third heart to his king and a fourth heart, knocking out
West's queen. South is in complete control: a diamond from West can be
ruffed and the clubs run while a spade to East's king gives the defence
their third and last trick.

52. KNOWN ATTITUDE

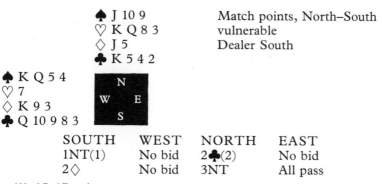

♠ J 10 9
♡ K Q 8 3
♢ J 5
♣ K 5 4 2

Match points, North–South
vulnerable
Dealer South

♠ K Q 5 4
♡ 7
♢ K 9 3
♣ Q 10 9 8 3

SOUTH	WEST	NORTH	EAST
1NT(1)	No bid	2♣(2)	No bid
2♢	No bid	3NT	All pass

(1) 15–17 points.
(2) No frills Stayman.

1. West led the ten of clubs, won by South's **jack**, *East discarding* ♠2.
2. South led ♢4: three–jack–**ace**.
3. East switched to the three of spades: seven–**queen**–nine.

HOW SHOULD WEST CONTINUE?

HOW THE PLAY WENT:

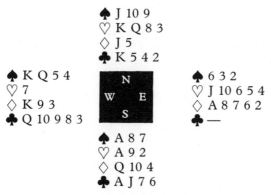

♠ J 10 9
♡ K Q 8 3
♢ J 5
♣ K 5 4 2

♠ K Q 5 4
♡ 7
♢ K 9 3
♣ Q 10 9 8 3

♠ 6 3 2
♡ J 10 6 5 4
♢ A 8 7 6 2
♣ —

♠ A 8 7
♡ A 9 2
♢ Q 10 4
♣ A J 7 6

Anxious not to give declarer a second spade trick, West continued with the queen of clubs at trick four; won by the king. The ♢5 went to the queen and king and again West played a top club, won by South's ace. East discarded a heart and a diamond on these club tricks. Declarer then played a heart to the king and a heart back to the ace, West discarding a spade.

The ♢Q was cashed, dummy shedding a heart, and a heart led to dummy. When West pitched a club, declarer played a club putting West on lead and forcing him to concede a second spade trick after all. 3NT made.

WHAT ERRORS, IF ANY, WERE COMMITTED?

Solution:
On the hand given, East could have defeated 3NT had he ducked the first round of diamonds or if West had risen with the king of diamonds and the second round of diamonds were ducked by East, but that was not easy to judge.

On the actual hand below, declarer made 3NT on the defence given and did not have to resort to any endplay. Nevertheless the defence could and should have beaten the contract.

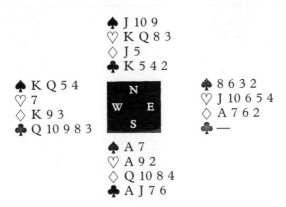

The given defence allows declarer to make nine tricks in comfort as the nine of diamonds drops on the third round giving declarer two diamond tricks to go with one spade, three hearts and three clubs.

Best defence defeats 3NT: ♣10 lead (normal), won by the jack as East discards ♠2; ♢4 to the jack and ace; ♠3–seven–queen wins; low spade back, dislodging the ace and now the defence has five available tricks as soon as the ♢K gains the lead. If South cashes three rounds of hearts, West discards one club and one diamond.

West can tell the ♠A will drop from East's carding. *Having already given attitude in spades* (with the ♠2), *East's next spade card should give the present count.* Thus when West sees the ♠3 at trick three, he can assess that East has three spades and South only a doubleton.

Where on the hand on the previous page East started with ♠ 6–3–2, his correct card after discarding the ♠2 at trick one was to return the ♠6, top from his remaining doubleton, again giving the present count. Then West would know that it would be futile to play a second spade and would have to try to disguise his holding as best he could.

53. MAMMY'S LITTLE BABY LOVES SHORTENIN', SHORTENIN'

♠ J 7 6 3
♡ 5
◇ Q 8 7 3
♣ A K 5 4

Teams, both sides vulnerable
Dealer South

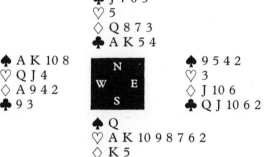

SOUTH	WEST	NORTH	EAST
4♡	Double	All pass	

♠ Q
♡ A K 10 9 8 7 6 2
◇ K 5
♣ 8 7

West led the king of spades, then the ace of diamonds and then the ace of spades. South ruffed the second spade.

HOW SHOULD SOUTH PROCEED?

HOW THE PLAY WENT:

♠ J 7 6 3
♡ 5
◇ Q 8 7 3
♣ A K 5 4

♠ A K 10 8   ♠ 9 5 4 2
♡ Q J 4   ♡ 3
◇ A 9 4 2   ◇ J 10 6
♣ 9 3   ♣ Q J 10 6 2

♠ Q
♡ A K 10 9 8 7 6 2
◇ K 5
♣ 8 7

1. ♠K led: three–five–queen.
2. ◇A led: three–six–five.
3. ♠A led: six–two–♡2.
4. ♡A cashed.
5. ♡K cashed.

Declarer conceded a heart. Making ten tricks.

WHAT ERRORS WERE MADE?

Solution:
As it happened, declarer failed in 4♡ doubled when the heart break was the worst possible, all four in West's hand. Yet declarer might have made his contract but for an early oversight. This was the actual hand:

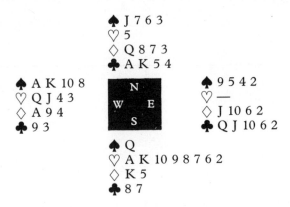

                       ♠ J 7 6 3
                       ♡ 5
                       ◇ Q 8 7 3
                       ♣ A K 5 4

♠ A K 10 8   ♠ 9 5 4 2
♡ Q J 4 3   ♡ —
◇ A 9 4   ◇ J 10 6 2
♣ 9 3   ♣ Q J 10 6 2

                       ♠ Q
                       ♡ A K 10 9 8 7 6 2
                       ◇ K 5
                       ♣ 8 7

Declarer should reason early that the only thing that could go wrong would be a 4–0 trump break, not all that far-fetched since West had no more than ♠A–K and ◇A for the double and there was no guarantee that even one of his spades would live. To have any chance against a 4–0 trump break, South has to reduce his trumps to K–10–9 and with three cards to go and West holding Q–J–4, South leads the ten forcing West on lead to surrender one of his two 'sure' trump tricks.

To achieve this South has to reduce his trump length by trumping four times. West's ace of spades provides the first ruff but the others have to be arranged, and declarer needs three entries to dummy. Thus to overcome a 4–0 break, South had to throw the ◇K under the ace at trick two so that the ◇Q could be used as an entry. The play would then go: ♠K; ◇A, South dropping the king; ♠A, South ruffing. ♡A, finding the grim news and then to make the hand South has to pick West's exact shape as he needs to know which of dummy's cards to ruff without getting overruffed. The winning continuation is: diamond to the queen; diamond ruff; club to the ace; spade ruff; club to the king; spade ruff. South then has the ending needed.

If South does make 4♡ doubled in that fashion, it would still be premature to taunt West, saying innocently: 'What did you have for your double?', for next time West may remember this debacle and instead of continuing with the ace of spades at trick three he might continue diamonds or lead a club, thus preventing South from being able to shorten himself sufficiently to achieve the trump endplay. When one appears to have unassailable trump tricks, one must not assist declarer in shortening his own trump holding. To reduce declarer's shortening capabilities, attack the entries in dummy.

54. SIGN OF THE TIMES

♠ A 9 7
♡ 7 6
◇ Q J 9 8 3
♣ K 10 3

Teams, East–West vulnerable
Dealer North

♠ 3 2
♡ A J 10 5 4
◇ K 5 4
♣ J 9 2

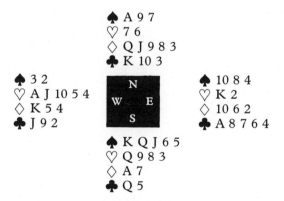

WEST	NORTH	EAST	SOUTH
	No bid	No bid	1♠
No bid	3◇(1)	No bid	4♠
No bid	No bid	No bid	

(1) Maximum pass, good 5+ diamond suit, 3-card spade support.

1. West led ♣2: seven–eight–**king**.
2. **Ace** of diamonds from South: four–three–two.
3. Seven of diamonds from South: **king**–eight–ten.

HOW SHOULD WEST CONTINUE?

HOW THE PLAY WENT:

♠ A 9 7
♡ 7 6
◇ Q J 9 8 3
♣ K 10 3

♠ 3 2
♡ A J 10 5 4
◇ K 5 4
♣ J 9 2

♠ 10 8 4
♡ K 2
◇ 10 6 2
♣ A 8 7 6 4

♠ K Q J 6 5
♡ Q 9 8 3
◇ A 7
♣ Q 5

At trick four West led the two of clubs, the ten forcing the ace. East returned the king of hearts and West won the next heart but declarer had the balance, ruffing the third heart high.

WHAT ERRORS WERE COMMITTED?

Solution:
Declarer in fact made his contract when West missed an inference from East's carding. This was the actual hand:

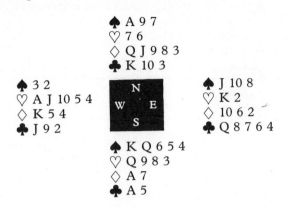

```
              ♠ A 9 7
              ♡ 7 6
              ◇ Q J 9 8 3
              ♣ K 10 3
♠ 3 2                        ♠ J 10 8
♡ A J 10 5 4      N          ♡ K 2
◇ K 5 4       W       E      ◇ 10 6 2
♣ J 9 2           S          ♣ Q 8 7 6 4
              ♠ K Q 6 5 4
              ♡ Q 9 8 3
              ◇ A 7
              ♣ A 5
```

   To defeat 4♠, the defence has to be very sharp. At trick four, in with the ◇K, West needs to switch to a low heart to East's king. East returns the two of hearts and the third heart from West promotes a trump trick for East. Declarer cannot do better by trying the diamond finesse for even if it works, he is faced with four heart losers and the trump lead has precluded the possibility of trumping hearts in dummy.

   If West finds the low heart switch to the king and a heart comes back, West should have no trouble finding the third heart. If East began with the ace of clubs, (and three hearts or is unable to obtain a promotion), East would have cashed the ♣A before returning the heart to avoid any mistake by West.

   West should be guided to the heart switch by East's *ten* of diamonds at trick three. On the ace of diamonds East followed with the two, indicating an odd number of diamonds, obviously three (with 10–2, East would play the ten then the two). Thus East's ten on the next round of diamonds is an unusual card and should be treated as a suit-preference signal for the higher suit, hearts. With no special desire for hearts, East would play the two then the six. As East could not be asking for a heart switch without the king, West should take care to play low rather than to lead the ace first.

55. UNDERWRITING THE PLAY

♠ A 10 9 3
♡ Q 6
◇ J 10 5 4
♣ J 5 4

Rubber bridge, East–West vulnerable
Dealer West

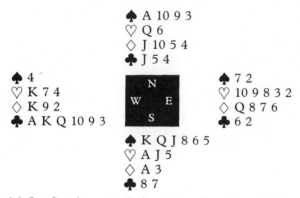

WEST	NORTH	EAST	SOUTH
1♣	No bid	No bid	2♠
No bid	4♠	All pass	

♠ K Q J 8 6 5
♡ A J 5
◇ A 3
♣ 8 7

1. West led the **king** of clubs: four–six–seven.
2. West led the **queen** of clubs: five–two–eight.
3. West led the ace of clubs: jack–*two of hearts*–**ruffed** by South.
4. South played **king** of spades: four–three–two.
5. South played queen of spades: *seven of hearts from West* . . .

HOW SHOULD SOUTH CONTINUE WITH THE PLAY?

HOW THE PLAY WENT:

```
              ♠ A 10 9 3
              ♡ Q 6
              ◇ J 10 5 4
              ♣ J 5 4
♠ 4                          ♠ 7 2
♡ K 7 4              N        ♡ 10 9 8 3 2
◇ K 9 2         W        E    ◇ Q 8 7 6
♣ A K Q 10 9 3       S        ♣ 6 2
              ♠ K Q J 8 6 5
              ♡ A J 5
              ◇ A 3
              ♣ 8 7
```

At trick five South overtook the queen of spades with dummy's ace and led the queen of hearts, ducked to West's king. West exited with a heart and declarer eventually lost a diamond trick.

WHAT ERRORS WERE COMMITTED?

AFTER TRICK THREE, IF YOU ARE GIVEN THAT THE KING OF HEARTS IS WITH WEST AND THAT THE DIAMOND HONOURS ARE SPLIT, WHAT DIAMOND HOLDING WITH WEST GUARANTEES SUCCESS IN FOUR SPADES?

Solution:

Declarer's best chance in 4♠ is the heart finesse but there are a few minor additional chances and declarer should explore these before resorting ultimately to the heart play. One possibility is that West has K–Q bare of diamonds and South can play ace and another diamond, endplaying West.

Ace and another diamond would also have worked on the actual hand via a curious position:

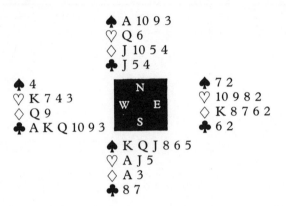

```
              ♠ A 10 9 3
              ♡ Q 6
              ◇ J 10 5 4
              ♣ J 5 4
  ♠ 4            N          ♠ 7 2
  ♡ K 7 4 3               ♡ 10 9 8 2
  ◇ Q 9       W     E     ◇ K 8 7 6 2
  ♣ A K Q 10 9 3   S      ♣ 6 2
              ♠ K Q J 8 6 5
              ♡ A J 5
              ◇ A 3
              ♣ 8 7
```

After three rounds of clubs and two rounds of trumps, declarer plays the ace of diamonds and another diamond. If West plays nine of diamonds and then the queen, he is endplayed if left on lead and if East overtakes with the king, dummy has two winners for heart discards. If West plays the queen first to unblock, then on the next round South again ducks in dummy when West's nine appears and the defence is left with the same dilemma.

In addition to finding West with K–Q bare, ace and another diamond will work for Q–9 or K–9 of diamonds with West. However, a low diamond away from the ace would work for K or Q singleton, as well as K–Q bare. South would have to choose whether to play West for a specific doubleton or a singleton honour. When West turns up with a singleton spade, the doubleton diamond holding is more likely.

56. GET THE MESSAGE

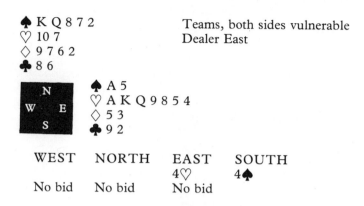

♠ K Q 8 7 2
♡ 10 7
◇ 9 7 6 2
♣ 8 6

♠ A 5
♡ A K Q 9 8 5 4
◇ 5 3
♣ 9 2

Teams, both sides vulnerable
Dealer East

WEST	NORTH	EAST	SOUTH
		4♡	4♠
No bid	No bid	No bid	

1. West led the three of hearts: seven–**queen**–jack.
2. East continued with the king of hearts: ♠4–♡6–♡**10**.
3. South led the nine of spades: three–king–**ace**.

HOW SHOULD EAST CONTINUE?

HOW THE PLAY WENT:

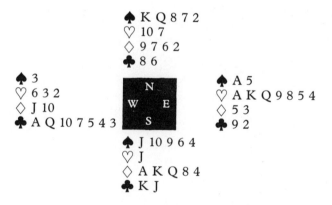

♠ K Q 8 7 2
♡ 10 7
◇ 9 7 6 2
♣ 8 6

♠ 3
♡ 6 3 2
◇ J 10
♣ A Q 10 7 5 4 3

♠ A 5
♡ A K Q 9 8 5 4
◇ 5 3
♣ 9 2

♠ J 10 9 6 4
♡ J
◇ A K Q 8 4
♣ K J

At trick four, East switched to the nine of clubs, jack, queen. West cashed the ace of clubs and declarer was one down.

WHAT ERRORS, IF ANY, WERE COMMITTED?

Solution:
The actual hand arose in the 1979 playoff to select the Australian Open Team. At the table, East did switch to a club at trick four but this was not a success as the complete hand was:

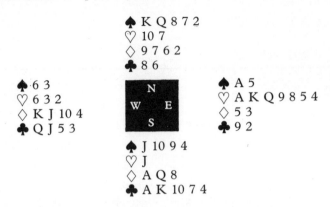

♠ K Q 8 7 2
♡ 10 7
◇ 9 7 6 2
♣ 8 6

♠ 6 3   ♠ A 5
♡ 6 3 2   ♡ A K Q 9 8 5 4
◇ K J 10 4   ◇ 5 3
♣ Q J 5 3   ♣ 9 2

♠ J 10 9 4
♡ J
◇ A Q 8
♣ A K 10 7 4

South's 4♠ over 4♡ would not be everyone's choice but Tim Seres justified the bid when he brought home 4♠ very prettily. The ♡3 went to the queen and South ruffed the ♡K, West following with ♡6. A spade went to East's ace and when East switched to a club, South won ♣A, ♣K and ruffed a club with the ♠7. A trump to hand drew the remaining trumps and another club was ruffed.

With his last club now established, declarer led a diamond to his *eight*, endplaying West who had to return a diamond into the A–Q or concede a ruff-and-discard.

That pretty play would not have materialised had East found the correct defence of a diamond at trick four. The clue to this play was West's *six* of hearts at trick two. *When partner's attitude and count is known*, idle cards should be used for suit-preference purposes. Thus if West would have wanted a club through, he would have followed with an *abnormal two* of hearts at trick two. By following with the six, the *normal* continuation of M.U.D., he was indicating either that he wanted diamonds or that he had no special preference for clubs. Either way East ought to have led a diamond.

For those partnerships that lead lowest from three cards, regardless of their value, West would have led the two of hearts initially but his second heart would again have been the six, in this case an abnormal card requesting a diamond through declarer. If East had led a diamond, South would have failed: if he ducked the diamond to West's ten, West would have had to exit with a spade but that would have been clear enough.

57. HOIST BY HIS OWN PETARD

♠ J 4 3
♡ A 8
◇ A J 10 4
♣ 9 7 3 2

Teams bridge, both sides vulnerable
Dealer South

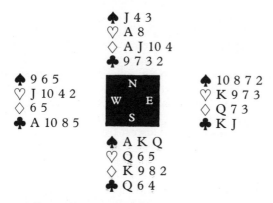

SOUTH	WEST	NORTH	EAST
1NT(1)	No bid	3NT	All pass

♠ A K Q
♡ Q 6 5
◇ K 9 8 2
♣ Q 6 4

(1) 15–17 points.
1. West led the two of hearts: eight–**king**–five.
2. East returned the three of hearts: six–four–**ace**.

HOW SHOULD SOUTH CONTINUE:

(a) AGAINST WEAK OPPOSITION?

(b) AGAINST STRONG OPPONENTS?

HOW THE PLAY WENT:

```
              ♠ J 4 3
              ♡ A 8
              ◇ A J 10 4
              ♣ 9 7 3 2
♠ 9 6 5                      ♠ 10 8 7 2
♡ J 10 4 2                   ♡ K 9 7 3
◇ 6 5                        ◇ Q 7 3
♣ A 10 8 5                   ♣ K J
              ♠ A K Q
              ♡ Q 6 5
              ◇ K 9 8 2
              ♣ Q 6 4
```

Shrugging his shoulders, declarer at trick three cashed the ace of diamonds and led the jack of diamonds: low, low, low. Once the ◇Q was picked up, declarer had nine tricks.

WERE THERE ANY ERRORS?

Solution:
In practice declarer was not so lucky with the position of the queen of diamonds and he went one down on this layout:

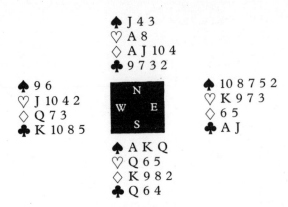

<pre>
                ♠ J 4 3
                ♡ A 8
                ◇ A J 10 4
                ♣ 9 7 3 2
  ♠ 9 6   ♠ 10 8 7 5 2
  ♡ J 10 4 2   N   ♡ K 9 7 3
  ◇ Q 7 3   W   E   ◇ 6 5
  ♣ K 10 8 5   S   ♣ A J
                ♠ A K Q
                ♡ Q 6 5
                ◇ K 9 8 2
                ♣ Q 6 4
</pre>

The hand essentially boils down to locating the queen of diamonds. Playing on the club suit is far too dangerous. However, declarer can do better than take just a 50–50 guess as to the queen's location.

Against weak opponents, declarer should cash the three top spades before tackling the diamonds. That may not help him at all but sometimes the distribution of the spade suit will be revealed. It is clear from the first two tricks that hearts are 4–4. If on playing the spades, declarer discovers that spades are 5–2 or 6–1 he will be able to place one opponent with nine or ten cards in the majors. On the hand above East turns up with nine major cards. Logically therefore declarer should play West for the queen of diamonds.

Against strong opponents, however, there is a better move available as the spades will be 4–3 most of the time and declarer will be little wiser. Here declarer should come to hand with the ♠A at trick 3 and lead the nine of diamonds. This move may turn West's expertise against him for a strong West will insert the queen of diamonds from Q–x or even Q–x–x, playing South for 9–x or 9–x–x in diamonds and trying to cut declarer off from the use of dummy's diamonds. If after all, West plays low on the nine of diamonds, declarer can still rise with the ace of diamonds and lead the jack to finesse against East.

The point is a subtle one and is valid only against the top echelon of defenders.